T0268985

Ministry Proverbs

Lessons Learned for Leading Congregations

N. Graham Standish

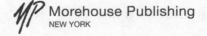
Morehouse Publishing
NEW YORK

Copyright © 2016 by N. Graham Standish

All rights reserved. No part of this book may be reproduced, stored in a retrieval system, or transmitted in any form or by any means, electronic or mechanical, including photocopying, recording, or otherwise, without the written permission of the publisher.

Unless otherwise noted, the Scripture quotations contained herein are from the New Revised Standard Version Bible, copyright © 1989 by the Division of Christian Education of the National Council of Churches of Christ in the U.S.A. Used by permission. All rights reserved.

Morehouse Publishing, 19 East 34th Street, New York, NY 10016
Morehouse Publishing is an imprint of Church Publishing Incorporated.
www.churchpublishing.org

Cover design by Jennifer Kopec, 2 Pug Design
Typeset by Rose Design

Library of Congress Cataloging-in-Publication Data

Names: Standish, N. Graham, 1959– author.
Title: Ministry proverbs : lessons learned for leading congregations / N. Graham Standish.
Description: New York : Morehouse Publishing, 2016. | Includes bibliographical references.
Identifiers: LCCN 2016009679 (print) | LCCN 2016010316 (ebook) | ISBN 9780819232823 (pbk.) | ISBN 9780819232830 (ebook)
Subjects: LCSH: Standish, N. Graham, 1959—Quotations. | Christian leadership—Quotations, maxims, etc.
Classification: LCC BV652.1 .S684 2016 (print) | LCC BV652.1 (ebook) | DDC
    253—dc23
LC record available at http://lccn.loc.gov/2016009679

Printed in the United States of America

DEDICATION

To Richard Bass, Diana Butler Bass, and Beth Gaede.
You three have had a huge impact on my writing
and my thinking, and I deeply appreciate it.

Introduction

YEARS AGO I DISCOVERED a particular biblical proverb that has become foundational for me ever since. I don't remember how I came upon it. It may have been part of a retreat exercise and discussion. It might have been used by a professor to emphasize a point or in a book to support an idea. Or it may have been used for a sermon. I don't remember, but I do remember that the moment I heard it or read it, it capsulized an approach to life that I've tried to instill ever since: "Trust in the Lord with all your heart, and do not rely on your own insight. In all your ways acknowledge him, and he will make straight your paths" (Proverbs 3:5–6).

The proverb was so simple, so elegant, so piercing, and so brilliant all at the same time. In a simple way it profoundly captured a whole approach to life, work, ministry, and faith—trust God, focus on what God wants, and everything will turn out okay. By applying it to my life, I've experienced its truth over and over. Whenever I've tried to really rely on God and God's insights, things seem to straighten out.

There's a reason both biblical and folk proverbs have had such an enduring power for hundreds and thousands of years. Proverbs provide simple wisdom that has a profound effect on life. The biblical book of Proverbs has had such an impact. Millions throughout the ages have benefitted from its wisdom. Applying these proverbs to our lives can make all the difference between living a self-focused, struggling life, and a life filled with meaning and blessing.

What makes proverbs so powerful? It's their unique combination of simplicity and profundity. Like simple melodies that stick in our heads and have significant emotional impact on us, proverbs are phrases that run though our heads and have a significant intuitive impact. They pop into our heads in times of struggle, uncertainty, and complexity, guiding us to do what's right.

Over the years I've realized that not only did I resonate with a number of proverbs, I was developing my own in regards to leading a congregation. These ministry proverbs had the ability to guide me when times were uncertain, difficult, or hard to think through in my ministry. These weren't proverbs I necessarily picked up from others, but they were simple phrases that I seemed to spontaneously develop over time in the face of certain challenges. I would have a difficult experience, and in the midst of it a phrase would come into my head, giving me guidance. Or afterward, as I reflected on what went well in a situation, a simple phrase would somehow capture what was right. Sometimes the phrase was a thought. Sometimes I just said it while responding to someone else, and the phrase stuck. Periodically the phrases coalesced as I drove my car or took a walk and reflected on a situation.

For instance, one of the first proverbs I seemingly spontaneously developed was one you'll see in this book, which is Proverb 9: "When a person complains anonymously, find out whether the person is the tip of an iceberg, or just a chip of ice."

The proverb popped out of my mouth in a conversation early in my ministry as pastor of Calvin Presbyterian Church. Our secretary had pulled me aside one morning to share a complaint from a church member. I don't remember the complaint anymore, but I do remember my secretary telling me that the member wanted to remain anonymous. I asked her to tell me anyway. She said that the member made her promise not to. I replied that she has to remember that her job was to be my secretary and the secretary to our staff, not secretary to the whole church. So her responsibility was to us, not the members. I also told her that not all complaints are equal because those that come from constant complainers who only cared about themselves weren't as serious as those from church leaders who deeply care about the church. I then said, "Look, if you don't let me know who it was, I can't determine if the complaint is the tip of an iceberg that can sink the ship, or a chip of ice that will melt away."

Eventually she told me who it was. It was a chip. The complaint was from a constant complainer who had very little traction in the congregation. There were others in the church who, if the complaint had been from them, would have gotten a visit from me. I wouldn't have told them I knew about their complaint, but I would have given them ample opportunity to share their complaint with me personally. Even if they didn't share their complaint, I would have taken the complaint (keeping the name of the complaining person confidential) to an appropriate committee or board, or even a staff member, if the complaint had been about the staff member. Since then this wisdom has always stuck with me. Whenever I hear complaining I immediately try to determine if it is the tip of an iceberg that can damage the church, or just a chip of ice that will melt with time.

The following is a collection of sixty proverbs that seemed to have spontaneously popped out of my experiences, and that now guide me throughout my ministry. I've been collecting them and writing them down for years. Over the past few years I began to share some of these proverbs with others, who seemed to benefit from them. This is how I decided to write them down. Also, I began to post them on a Ministry Proverbs page on Facebook, sharing one every two to four weeks. Over the course of eight months, hundreds of followers not only seemed to benefit from them but shared them with others. This is what led me to think about publishing them as part of a book.

What you'll find in this book are these proverbs. I've tried to write them down in simple yet memorable ways. Each proverb is intended to target a particular aspect of church ministry that is difficult to navigate. The idea is that if you can remember the simple phrases during these times, they will help you find a healthier way to get through them. In some cases, they may even help you thrive through them. Following each proverb are four to seven paragraphs exploring what each proverb means. You'll probably find that some really stick with you, some will get you to think, some will actually help you change your approach to ministry and mission, and some you'll just go, "Eh." But that's the nature of proverbs. Proverbs hit you with wisdom where you are struggling or need to hear God.

There are many ways to use these proverbs. They can be used personally by pastors and lay leaders as weekly meditations for learning how to lead a church to greater health. They can be used as monthly reflections for church boards and committees as a way of sparking discussions among leaders. They can be used among pastors who gather weekly or monthly to have discussions, prayer, and support. Here are some ways to potentially use the proverbs in groups:

- Divide the proverbs into twelve groupings of five proverbs to be read beforehand and discussed once a month for a twelve-month study by church boards, committees, or other groups.
- Divide the proverbs into six groupings of ten proverbs to be read beforehand and discussed once a month for a six-month study by church boards, committees, or other groups.
- Use for personal reflection as a five-day a week, twelve week program.

However you choose to use them, my hope and prayer is that you will find them as helpful as I have.

Ministry Proverbs

1. We are only responsible for our efforts. God is responsible for the results. So be responsible for your part, and let God be responsible for God's part. Wisdom comes in learning to tell the difference.

2. The secret to prayer is to pray specifically for what we want, but to accept faithfully what we get.

3. Don't try to keep disgruntled people in your church, keep the gruntled people. Disgruntled people spread disgruntlement like a virus. So let them go, and let them take their grunts with them.

4. People seek surprise, not stagnation. So why do we so often offer stagnation rather than surprise in worship?

5. Be like water in your leadership, not like lava. When we are like water, we overcome all obstacles, but when we are like lava we become obstacles.

6. When trying to transform a church, the most important thing is making people feel safe. If they don't feel safe, they will resist and growl. But if they feel safe, they will follow and grow.

7. Seeking shortcuts usually gets us lost, and when we are lost, things always take longer.

8. Avoiding problems usually creates bigger problems. Avoiding problems is the result of avoiding pain. And avoiding pain eventually increases pain. So deal with problems before they become a pain.

9. When a person complains anonymously, find out whether the person is the tip of an iceberg, or just a chip of ice.

10. Criticism creates stagnation, but praise stimulates creativity.

11. Even if we will only lead a church for three years, lead as though we will be there for thirty.

12. If a church won't say to God, "Thy will be done," then God will let their will be done, even if it leads to their demise.

13. The difference between God being nowhere and God being now here is the space we create for God.

14. Church, as well as faith, is about relationships, not rightness or righteousness, because in the end true righteousness comes from right relationships.

15. In life and ministry, we can't get others to care about us by trying to get others to care about us. We only get others to care about us when we spend our lives caring about others.

16. We are ultimately called to apostleship, not discipleship. Discipleship is a stage on the way to apostleship. To be a disciple is to be a student, but to be an apostle is to be a sent servant.

17. When making a change in a church that people think is wrong, try it long enough to determine whether it is wrong because it's actually wrong or because it just feels wrong.

18. When trying to determine whether to engage in a new ministry or mission, focus on "what are we called to do" rather than "what should we do."

19. Treat all people as though they are forgiven people, not sinful people, because that's what they are.

20. When you love and praise people, you help them grow. When you criticize them, you make them wither. When you love and praise churches, you help them grow. When you criticize them, you make them wither.

21. Church life requires balance, and when there is no balance in the church, the people fall.

22. Don't become so theologically pure in your ministry that it becomes spiritually foolish.

23. You can't do anything about things you can't do anything about, but you can do things about things you can do something about. So focus on what you can do something about, and let go of what you can't do anything about.

24. If you've bitten off more than you can chew as a church, spit it out and take smaller bites. You don't have to do everything all at once.

25. Discernment means trusting in a plan that God never fully reveals and that we never fully understand, but trusting God to take care of it all in the end anyway.

26. In the event of a church or leadership crisis, get your own oxygen first before assisting others.

27. When leading a church, learn the great secret that "everything matters; nothing matters."

28. Churches constantly battle entropy, which leads to apathy, which leads to atrophy. Churches can only overcome entropy with spiritual energy. If they restore the Spirit, they can multiply; if not, they will simply gentrify.

29. Churches become healthy when they know "why" they do "what" they do. When what we do is based on a clear "why," we act with purpose. When we don't know why we do what we do, we lose our focus.

30. When doing pastoral care we need to ask, "Am I here simply to listen, or to help solve a problem?" If we merely listen when a problem needs to be solved, we increase helplessness. If we try to solve a problem when someone just wants to be heard, we increase frustration.

31. If the church isn't growing, it's dying, because the nature of life is to grow. And once it starts dying, the only answer is to prune and nourish: prune what is dying, and nourish what may grow.

32. We should seek simplicity and naturality in all that we do in a church. There is a natural way of being simple, and a simple way of being natural. And when churches become more naturally simple, they grow.

33. All churches create self-fulfilling prophecies about themselves. The question is what kind they will create: a prophecy of struggle, turmoil, and decline, or one of love, passion, and growth?

34. When we preach, if we are not focused on transforming people, we merely inform people. And when we merely inform people, the best we can be is merely interesting. But when we focus on forming people, we can transform them.

35. Ministry is about loving others, but love needs boundaries. When we have no boundaries, we can easily be manipulated because manipulators love to manipulate those who love.

36. Love and trust are the most important qualities of healthy churches. When congregations feel loved and trusted by pastors, they can accomplish almost anything. When they feel unloved and distrusted, they will struggle, snipe, and stagnate.

37. The church needs to tell people *why* they believe more than *what* they believe. Sharing *why* tells our story and invites people to experience God. Sharing *what* we believe merely invites them to decide whether or not they agree with our dogma.

38. Don't confuse inspiration and stimulation. Inspiration comes from connecting people with God. Stimulation is all about getting people excited. Settling for stimulation ends up relying on manipulation. Striving for inspiration ends up leading people to transformation.

39. What we strive for is what we get. If we strive for numbers, we get a church of people who like to follow a crowd. If

we strive merely to survive, we get a church of people who only seek self-preservation. But if we strive for God, we get a church full of people who yearn for God.

40. If we merely seek leaders with good organizing, teaching, accounting, or property skills, why then complain that our members are uninspired? If we seek leaders with a yearning for God, they will lead others to be inspired.

41. If a congregation is whining like a bunch of babies, it usually means that we need to help them take baby steps.

42. Too often pastors become disappointed because their churches aren't more mature. But if their churches were more mature, they wouldn't need a pastor. So pastors need to remember that their role is to lead churches to maturity, just as a parent's role is to lead children to maturity.

43. Just because someone says something offensive to us doesn't mean we have to be offended. Just because someone rejects us doesn't mean we have to reject her or him. Treating people in kind generally makes us less kind. Being a leader means treating people better than they treat us in order to help them become better people.

44. When people say they are "spiritual but not religious," they are rightly telling the church that we are "religious but not spiritual." The answer for both is to become spiritual *and* religious.

45. When we get caught up in the darkness of life, we generally only notice God's absence. But when we look for light, we discover God's presence. Lead people to look for light, especially in darkness.

46. Remember that no matter how much the dogs bark, the mail gets delivered anyway. Learn to distinguish between the members who bark and those who bite.

47. How we make decisions is much more important than what decisions we make. When decisions are made communally, respectfully, and prayerfully, they lead us to

serve God. When they aren't, even the best decisions can become divisive.

48. Every ministry has a lifespan. When we force dying ministries to stay alive, we also prevent new ministries from being resurrected from their death. Learn to let ministries and missions die when they need to, so that new ministries and missions can be born in their place.

49. Never work harder than our members. If we do, they'll let us do all the work.

50. Just because we are certain doesn't make us right, but it certainly can make us self-righteous.

51. We never regret a wise decision, but we always regret the selfish one.

52. If the church can't live without us, then it's probably on its way to dying with us.

53. Whether we like it or not, pastors are often expected to be the most mature persons in a room, which means that other leaders may treat us poorly while treating problem people well. Pastors have to learn how to respond to the most painful situations in spiritually mature ways.

54. Visionary leaders see the horizon, figure out how to get there, and forge a path for others. Ordinary leaders either only see the path and get lost, or only point to the horizon while going nowhere.

55. Some pastors and churches are called to do seeker evangelism. Some are called to do depth evangelism. Some are called to do hospice care. Some are called to do birthing. We need to be sure that we know what our leadership calling is.

56. Beware of mission creep because once your mission starts creeping, it slows your ministry to a crawl.

57. Learn the five attributes of great chefs, and turn them into the five attributes of great pastors and leaders:

(1) They always use fresh ingredients. (2) They work hard together behind the scenes to make it look easy. (3) They are finicky about cleanliness. (4) They always strive to be hospitable and welcoming. (5) They are passionate about feeding others.

58. Healthy churches need to be both goal-oriented and God-oriented. Being goal-oriented means we see where we are going and what steps need to be taken to get there. Being God-oriented means we pay attention to where God is calling us to go so that we become goal-oriented in seeking God's orientation.

59. We can only think things through theologically and liturgically if we start by thinking things through spiritually and psychologically, which is where we create the possibility for a deep encounter with God in worship.

60. Good leadership means being able to be obsessive, improvising, and laid back all at the same time. Real wisdom comes with knowing when to be what.

Proverb 1.

We are only responsible for our efforts. God is responsible for the results. So be responsible for your part, and let God be responsible for God's part. Wisdom comes in learning to tell the difference.

WHAT IS YOUR PART IN MINISTRY? What's God's part? Do you confuse the two? Can you tell the difference?

I think that most of us in ministry, whether clergy or laity, confuse what we're responsible for and what God is responsible for. We tend to think everything is up to us, and that God is judging our efforts and results, as though success will open the pearly gates and failure will close them.

God only calls on us to do what we can—to give God our best efforts. Ultimately God is responsible for the results. If what we do is really trying to please God, to serve God, and to do what we sense God wants, it opens a conduit for God's grace to grow. I learned this lesson from the nineteenth-century Quaker mystic, Hannah Whitall Smith, who said,

> To sum it all up, then, what is needed for happy and effectual service is simply to put your work into the Lord's hands, and leave it there. Do not take it to Him in prayer, saying, "Lord, guide me; Lord, give me wisdom; Lord, arrange it for me," and then rise from your knees, and take the burden all back and try to guide and arrange for yourself. Leave it with the Lord; and remember that what you trust to Him you must not worry over nor feel anxious about. Trust and worry cannot go together. If your work is a burden it is because you are not trusting it to Him. But if you do trust it to Him you will surely find that the yoke He puts on you is easy, and the

burden He gives you to carry is light: and even in the midst of a life of ceaseless activity you shall "find rest to your soul."[1]

God wants our churches to do well. God wants us to do well. But we can't let God do well in our midst if we're constantly taking responsibility for everything. So do what you do well, and let God do what God does well. And bathe your efforts in prayer, asking God what is God's part and what is ours.

---

1. Hannah Whitall Smith, *The Christian's Secret of a Happy Life* (Grand Rapids, MI: Baker Book House Company, 1952): 202–03.

Proverb 2.

*The secret to prayer is to pray specifically for what
we want, but to accept faithfully what we get.*

P RAYER IS HARD FOR MANY REASONS, but chief among
them is that we don't know how specific we should get
in prayer. To what extent should we pray fervently for
what we want, and to what extent should we hedge our bets
and only pray for what God wants? There's more in this question than meets the eye.

There are a number of reasons we're reluctant to pray
specifically for what we want. What if we take a chance on
praying for a specific need and God doesn't give us what we
want? It feels like God is rejecting us. But is it really a rejec-
tion? Also, if we don't get what we pray for, does that confirm
our doubts that God even exists? Better to play it safe and
keep our fragile faith intact. What if it's wrong to ask for what
we want? Will God be irritated with us? Is it greedy to ask for
what we want? Isn't that putting ourselves in God's position
to assume that we know what's best? It's obvious that praying
specifically opens a big can of worms.

So, we don't typically pray with passion for healing.
Instead we pray for God's presence and strength. We don't
typically pray for God to help us financially. Instead we pray
for God's help and wisdom. We don't typically pray for God
to remove a thorn from our side. Instead, we pray for God to
give us endurance. We hold back our prayers.

Still, if we hold back in prayer, what do we do with
Jesus's teaching: "Ask, and it will be given you; search, and
you will find; knock, and the door will be opened for you.
For everyone who asks receives, and everyone who searches
finds, and for everyone who knocks, the door will be opened"

(Matthew 7:7–8)? Why would Jesus say this if he didn't mean it? The reality is that he says that we should pray specifically for what we want. In fact, we should pray passionately for what we want, whether it is for a job, healing, a relationship, financial help, or anything else. If you look in the Psalms, all of those prayers are passionate. That's our model.

Still, life is not really about God just giving us whatever we ask for. God isn't a genie in a lamp that we have to learn to rub just the right way to get what we want. We need to pray specifically for what we want, but also accept faithfully what God gives. This is a hard balance to keep. We want to be sure that if we pray specifically, we get what we specifically asked for. But that may not be God's will. We need to be sensitive enough to recognize how God may be answering our prayers. We may not get what we want, but generally we get what we need. So we need to passionately pray for what we want, and faithfully accept what we get.

This guidance isn't just for individuals. It is also for churches. Many churches and their members engage in *pro forma* prayers, going through the motions of praying, while secretly wondering if their prayers will be answered. They offer beautiful prayers—prayers that could be printed in books—but that doesn't mean their prayers are filled with faith. Churches should be rooted in a vibrant prayer that is filled with faith, which means praying specifically. These include prayers such as, "What are you calling us to budget for the following year?" and "How are you calling us to respond to this crisis?" It also means asking God to help us and our churches through financial distress. We need to pray passionately and often. But in the end, whether we are talking about churches or individuals, we need to accept the answers we receive: pray specifically for what we need, but accept faithfully what God gives in return.

Pray specifically. Accept faithfully.

Proverb 3.

Don't try to keep disgruntled people in your church, keep the gruntled people. Disgruntled people spread disgruntlement like a virus. So let them go, and let them take their grunts with them.

EVERY CHURCH HAS MEMBERS who become disgruntled. They don't like new music. They don't like old music. They don't like the new pastor. They didn't like the old pastor. They don't like new technology. They don't like the failure to embrace technology. I once had a member who walked through the handshake line each Sunday and complained that we weren't playing the organ enough. Three people behind him came a woman who complained most Sundays that we weren't playing enough contemporary Christian music. How could I alleviate one member's disgruntlement without increasing the other's?

It's so easy to get caught up in trying to make disgruntled people happy—to make them "gruntled." But the truth is that most disgruntled people never find happiness once they start "disgrunting." In fact, they start complaining to everyone around them, trying to find compatriots and conspirators. Their attempts to get traction eventually become divisive, especially as they begin to pile on the "disgrunts," adding more and more criticisms to their list of complaints. We don't make them happier by constantly meeting with them and finding out what we can do to help them. We don't reduce their disgruntlement, either. We just give them more power.

Of course, this is assuming that that the disgruntled people are just disgruntled. If the whole church becomes disgruntled, we may have to consider the possibility that we've put the "dis" in their disgruntlement.

Ultimately, we want people in our churches who look for what's right, rather than what's wrong; who see what's there, rather than what's missing. These are the people who can build a healthy church. These are the ones others want to be around, and who ultimately are good at finding and being God's presence. They are the gruntled.

It can be tremendously painful to let disgruntled people go, especially if they've been friends, supporters, or even leaders. But if we are serious about creating a healthy church, letting them go can help a church become healthier. As one pastor said to me about the loss of a member and large contributor who did nothing but complain, "When he left, I thought the waves would crash all around. Instead, the waters calmed, and nobody complained that he was gone. We realized that we were much healthier without him. We could now grow."

Proverb 4.

People seek surprise, not stagnation.
So why do we so often offer stagnation rather
than surprise in worship?

WHY, IN THE MAINLINE CHURCH, are we so scared of surprise? We try so hard to preserve what we've always done, and to sustain and maintain those who have always been there, that we ignore the human cry for surprise.

People crave surprise. I don't mean that we crave shock and startle. We like them only on special occasions, like riding roller coasters and watching horror flicks. What we crave are pleasant surprises that change our routines and give us new experiences and perspectives. You see the need for surprise everywhere. What makes dramas gripping? It's the fact that we don't know what is going to happen from scene to scene. Each scene starts out with something mundane, and ends up moving in a surprising direction. Then the ending gives us a whole new surprise as we find out who really murdered Mildred, who got voted onto the next round, whether they kissed, and whether or not the baby survived the surgery. What makes comedies funny is that the jokes are a pleasant surprise, as the familiar is twisted and taken in a whole new direction. Why is 6 afraid of 7? Because 7, 8, 9. (Say it out loud, you'll get it.)

Why do we love sports? Every game is a surprise. Why do we love travel? Every new vista is a new surprise. What makes our favorite songs favorites? First the melody catches us, then the bridge or refrain surprises us as the song is creatively transformed. Then, as we dig into the lyrics, we are surprised even more. Great art, literature, and even cartoons surprise us with fresh new perspectives that help us look at the world differently. So why do we choose stagnation over surprise in so much of our worship?

It's not as if everything must be a surprise. What makes pop songs popular is that they follow familiar formats, but then find ways to be surprising within that format. Detective shows always follow a consistent formula, but within that formula are multiple surprises. James Bond films always follow the same plot, but it's how he's going to escape that captures us. It's the interplay of the mundane and the imaginative that catches us. We don't have to make everything in worship a surprise. But the familiar needs to be laced with surprises.

For instance, does the sermon always follow the same structure? Aren't there ways to freshen it up with surprising new elements—throwing a baseball around to talk about the need to catch the Spirit; showing a picture of a Picasso painting to demonstrate how our perspectives on God can be a jumble; giving everyone an envelope with a special message from God ("I love you!") to be opened at the end of the sermon? Can't we vary the music so that there is a variety—not just one kind: either classical or contemporary? What if the church gave out balloons on Pentecost, just as we hand out palms on Palm Sunday? One reason people love Christmas and Easter so much is that there are surprises. The music is familiar yet different. The flowers make everything different, as do the candles and the way we dress.

The point is that often our worship lacks surprise, and so our churches lack surprise. And when they do, is it any surprise that people don't show up?

Proverb 5.

Be like water in your leadership, not like lava. When we are like water, we overcome all obstacles, but when we are like lava we become obstacles.

TOO OFTEN, WHEN CHURCH LEADERS hit an obstacle, they start leading like lava rather than like water. What's the difference? I want you to imagine that you are watching a stream of lava flowing down a mountain as it hits a deep trench, rimmed by massive boulders. The lava gets stuck. It can't flow over it, around it, or push it away. What happens to the lava? It cools, hardens, and becomes more rock—it builds a bigger obstacle.

In many ways too many church leaders and their churches become like hardened lava when they face problems. Every church encounters obstacles. Unfortunately, many church leaders, obsessed with the obstacles, keep pushing against the obstacle and stop momentum. When that happens they become like lava—cooling, hardening, and become obstacles themselves. For example, the church leaders may decide to replace the carpet in the sanctuary but end up divided over the cost, color, and kind of carpet to buy. The division becomes the obstacle, and both sides become so obsessed with their proposals that the church never moves forward. Each side freezes (which is what the hardening of lava really is), and if a pastor decides to resolve the decision by deciding, she or he becomes like lava too.

Pastors also become like lava when they become obsessed with a lack of passion among members or low attendance for programs, criticizing leaders for not doing enough. Members can become obsessed with pastors not performing better or staff not doing enough to grow the church. Whatever the issue, they all become like lava, hardening to the point where they create ever-bigger obstacles. And the red-hot anger that accompanies their frustration can make things worse, as those who try to intervene get burned.

Good leaders lead like water. Imagine that same mountain with a spring snowmelt flowing down its side. The water hits that same obstacle, but it doesn't stay put. No matter how big the obstacle is, the water either flows over it, around it, or it eventually erodes. Like water, when leaders encounter a division, they find new avenues to help members depolarize. Or they find alternatives that create new possibilities. Or they allow time to erode passions so that they can return to resolving the issues at a later time. For example, when faced with division over carpeting, they may overcome the problem by bringing parties together, emphasizing the idea that *what* decision is made isn't as important as *how* it is made. They emphasize relationships over results and encourage members to overcome their divisions. Or they may flow around the problem by looking for an alternative that brings members together. They may also decide to erode the problem by putting the issue aside for a time until dire need creates a better environment for cooperation.

Pastors who lead like water always look for possibilities and alternatives when they encounter obstacles. They don't become frozen, but let the obstacles help them become more creative in creating solutions. Obstacles become opportunities to create new rivers of ministry and mission.

Proverb 6.

When trying to transform a church, the most important thing is making people feel safe. If they don't feel safe, they will resist and growl. But if they feel safe, they will follow and grow.

THE REALITY IS THAT MANY, if not most, churches fear change. They want the church to be a stable point, an anchor, in a rapidly changing world. They face changes constantly at work, whether it's the demands of overbearing bosses, a competitive workplace, a cutthroat marketplace, the withering of grants and funding, or the fact that coworkers come and go. They face changes at home, whether it is the moving of children through different stages, marriages through different phases, or the chapters of life through different pages. Their health changes, their hair changes, their bodies change, their homes change, technology changes, music changes, their lives change. There are so many changes in life that it is hard to keep up. For example, the same people who used to be on the cutting edge of technology in college, having the best turntable and speakers, now feel intimidated by their phones.

Many, if not most, members hope that church will be the place that stays constant, steady, and that connects to an earlier, simpler, better time. But churches have to change. Otherwise what happens is exactly what is happening to the mainline church right now: they remain stuck in some sort of time warp where they have more in common with the mid-twentieth century than with the demands of the twenty-first century. Then they wonder why the young people stay away. Those young people never experienced that long ago golden age. People today don't need a church rooted in the 1950s, 1960s, or 1970s. They need a church that helps them navigate the demands of the new millennium, which may mean adapting to, and adopting many of, the changes of the twenty-first century while still being rooted in the teachings of the first-century church.

When we get down to the basics of leading a church in the twenty-first century, which we are already well into, we have to come to terms with the fact that the main reason people don't want their churches to change is that they are afraid. They are afraid that a changing church will also mean the loss of their values, their belief systems, and their traditions. Nobody wants to take these away, but we do need to apply them in a new way in a new age.

Leading a church through all of this uncertainty requires leaders who can help members feel safe in times of transformation. We need church leaders who can point to what's possible and make it feel simple to accomplish. We need leaders who can overcome members' survival instincts, which lead them to cower in a corner and growl, protecting what little they have, and to help them come out and grow. This is not an easy task because it requires leaders who have enough personal strength to withstand criticism, anger, and resistance to keep members moving forward toward the future, rather than retreating with them into the past. Too many leaders let their churches lead them backward, which means that they really aren't leaders.

The reality is that the members who are most afraid of change will never help us leaders feel safe. That's not their role. They see their role as protecting what was. To lead means to project what can be, and to protect them as they move tentatively toward the possible. To lead means to help people feel safe, even if we are terribly anxious about the prospect that we may fail. No leader has ever moved people forward without personal doubts, anxieties, and trepidation, and without a risk of failure. But the great ones stay calm, stay focused, and help people feel safe in the same way we help our kids grow by making them feel safe.

It's not the growls that matter. It's the growth.

Proverb 7.

*Seeking shortcuts usually gets us lost, and when
we are lost, things always take longer.*

T HIS PROVERB SHOULD BE OBVIOUS, but it's not. Too
often what short-circuits church health, church growth,
church ministry, and church mission is leaders seeking
shortcuts to whatever it is they're trying to accomplish. When
things aren't going well in churches, too often the leadership
spirals down into a whole series of shortcuts that make things
worse and cause churches to lose their way.

An example: For years our church had a terrible damp-
ness and mold problem in our basement. Every summer the
basement floors were covered with a glaze of water, causing
mold to grow in the preschool carpets. We had to replace
these numerous times, and even when we didn't, we had to
pay for them to be professionally cleaned. We tried to prevent
the problem by installing a number of dehumidifiers, but they
were just fingers in the dike.

When we did a massive renovation a few years ago we
discovered the source of the problem. Twenty years earlier
the church had decided to turn part of the basement into a
youth room. To do so, they took out window well windows,
filled the wells in with dirt, replaced the windows with plywood, and put drywall over them. They didn't want to pay
the cost of doing things right to create a watertight seal.
Unbeknownst to them the walls seeped behind the drywall
in the spring and summer, and water pooled on the floor. To
take care of the seepage they installed a sump pump behind a
wall under a stairwell. Four years before our construction, the
pump short-circuited and burned out, which no one noticed
because we didn't know it was there. The ones who installed

the pump had died or moved away. The workers told us we were lucky because it could have burned the church down. During renovation we discovered the burned-out pump, the plywood window replacements, and the source of our problems. By taking a shortcut to save money on covering the windows, the church ended up having to buy dehumidifiers, replace expensive carpets several times, buy a sump pump, and risked burning down the church. The $60 shortcut probably cost the church over $2,000 in the ensuing years and created many problems.

This example is just a microcosm of the kinds of shortcuts churches, pastors, and leaders take. For instance, in seeking church officers and board members, churches often settle for who will say "yes" rather than taking the time to look for someone with spiritual depth and leadership skills. They look for warm bodies rather than good leaders. In conducting meetings, committee and board members often care more about how quickly the meetings can end rather than the quality of the decisions made. Even in worship the focus is often on how close to noon the service can be over, rather than on whether or not people have actually experienced God. We seek short services, short sermons, short meetings, and shortcuts. Yet somehow we want these shortcuts to produce long-lasting, positive results. Unfortunately, they tend to lead to long-term problems. They get in the way of spiritual ministry and missional growth. They lead the church to lose its way.

Churches that do well make sure they take the time to do things well. They generally take the long way around. When members join the church, they ask them to take a number of classes over weeks, even months, rather than having them join quickly. They preach longer sermons that lead people to a deeper faith. Their services are somewhat longer because they seek quality in music, prayer, and worship in general. They take the time to plan their ministry and mission well. They take time in making decisions because they want to make sure they are making the right decision, not the quick decision.

They take their time to do things right, and as a result they do things right. In the end what they do is shorter overall because they only have to do things once. Think about it this way: Jesus took the time to do things right, even if it was painful, agonizing, and ultimately not what he wanted. He prayed that the Father would take the cup away from him, but in the end he said, "Not my will, but yours be done" (Luke 22:42). The result is a movement that has lasted 2,000 years and has 1.7 billion followers.

Proverb 8.

Avoiding problems usually creates bigger problems.
Avoiding problems is the result of avoiding pain.
And avoiding pain eventually increases pain. So deal
with problems before they become a pain.

TOO OFTEN WE CREATE MORE PAIN by avoiding pain. It's a natural consequence of our yearning for peace, calm, and security. Most people avoid conflict. Most people avoid pain. And the ones who don't are the ones we typically avoid because they inflict pain.

Why are so many churches in pain? A lot of it has to do with our expectations. We believe that churches should be harmonious places where there is no conflict or pain because they are where God resides. We have high expectations. The problem is that churches are often painful places precisely because humans naturally inflict pain on each other. We don't mean to, but when people rub against each other, they get rashes because they often act rashly. As I've often said, if you want a perfect church, get rid of the people. But if you get rid of the people, you no longer have a church. What a conundrum!

Churches exist precisely because people live painful lives. Human existence can both be precious and poisonous, as well as everything in between. We want churches to be pain free, but they are often painful. We are so quick to avoid pain that, like ignoring poison ivy in a garden, it spreads and becomes more pernicious than if we had just dealt with it when it was a small sprig.

The reality is that most of us don't know how to deal with small problems. Nor can we always tell whether they are really problems or just small irritants that should be ignored. So what do we do?

First, when faced with a potentially painful problem, *reflect on how the problem might grow if ignored*. But this must be done honestly, not anxiously. An anxious analysis would say, "Maybe if I don't do anything it will just go away." That's not a real reflection, that's anxious avoidance. A real reflection asks, "If I do nothing, will it grow? And if so, how large will it grow?" Will it eventually amount to nothing and remain a small issue, or will it grow to become divisive? The key to all problems is that the real ones divide people against God, and people against people, when unattended.

Second, *seek wise advice*. A mistake many in church leadership make is dealing with problems alone, which can create more problems when we act unwisely. Churches are intentional spiritual communities. We are meant to deal with issues together. So find someone in the community who has wisdom (don't just seek the person who agrees with you, or the person with power to help you). Let them help you sift through your options. If need be, take it to larger groups of wise people.

Third, deal with problem people *respectfully in a way filled with the Great Command*. When confronting a person or a situation, treat people the way we would want to be treated, even if they won't treat us the same way. Treating people respectfully in a crisis isn't weakness. It's strength. Always slow things down, resisting the urge to become angry or anxious. When in crisis, too many churches and their leaders are known for preaching the Great Command while then treating people with great contempt. When we become anxious or angry, we typically become defensive, and defensiveness drives others and us away from loving God as ourselves. The best way out of the Great Contempt is making sure that as our anger or anxiety grows, we pray and ask God to guide us. That is an act of loving God with all our minds, hearts, souls, and strength.

Finally, *always get ahead of the problem*. Too often, because we're fearful of conflict, we let the problems run away from us. Get ahead of the problems by making healthy plans to deal with them. Don't wait till the problems grow, but find a way to create systems that deal with issues before they grow.

An example: Years ago I was involved in a church where a two-person task force was created to take care of a leaky wall. Each one had his own idea about how the wall should be taken care of. They were divided and wanted to let the church board decide between them—to choose a winner. Big problem! Instead, I got them together and told them that I didn't care what they decided. I only cared about how they decided. And so I told them that I wouldn't let either solution come before the board. They had to come up with one together or not at all, which would mean that the wall would continue to leak. They eventually came up with a solution together, and it taught them that working together was more important than being in charge.

Proverb 9.

When a person complains anonymously,
find out whether the person is the tip of an iceberg,
or just a chip of ice.

I N EVERY CHURCH, PEOPLE PASS ALONG complaints to pastors. But they do so protecting the anonymity of the complainer, saying something like, "Pastor So-and-So, I just heard that one of our members, who wishes to remain anonymous, doesn't like the new class you're teaching. She believes that you're misusing the Bible, and she's very upset! I don't want to tell you who it is because she asked me not to. But I think it's important that you know."

What do you do? Do you change your class? Do you spend a class defending your beliefs? Do you preach a sermon about the evils of criticizing others, quoting from Philippians 2:3, "Do nothing from selfish ambition or conceit, but in humility regard others as better than yourselves"? Do you ignore the comment, hoping it will go away, while maintaining a genuine fear that this may be part of a larger revolt?

The dilemma all starts with a single question: *Is the complaint the tip of an iceberg, or just a chip of ice?* Who made the complaint really makes all the difference. In any church there are grumblers whose grousing ultimately makes no difference in the end. They are always going to find fault with pastors, church leaders, and other members no matter what. They will find fault in the pastor's classes, sermons, newsletter articles, pastoral presence, and leadership. Nothing the pastor does will be good enough. Perhaps the pastor will be measured against a heroic pastor from the church's past. Perhaps the pastor will be measured against a television preacher. Perhaps there is no measurement because these people just don't trust pastors. The fact is that whatever the reason for complaining, the other members know that these cranky pants are grumblers by nature, and so they avoid them. In other words, the complainers have no constituency—no group of people who follow their lead.

Also, in most churches there are people who just never understand the workings of a church, Christian theology, the spiritual life, or much of anything else. They complain because they don't understand much of anything. They may be heavily involved, but their lack of understanding means that they have no constituency. They complain out of ignorance.

The fact is that people like these are simply chips of ice. Their criticisms don't matter much because criticism is just their nature. They are like ice cubes floating in a drink. Over time their ability to chill the church melts away. They might have an immediate effect, but not a long-lasting one. If these are the kinds of people anonymously complaining, then whatever they have to say, reacting to their grumbles makes no positive difference. Defending ourselves, changing our classes, preaching about the evils of criticism will have no positive impact, and our responding actually can make things worse by making these chips of ice feel like powerful icebergs.

Meanwhile, there are many members who rarely complain. They support pastors, leaders, other members, and the church. They are always looking to build up the church. Often other members look up to them. They have a constituency. If they complain, we can be sure that they are the tips of icebergs. Their complaints are the visible tip of a whole series of submerged troubles. When a person like this complains, it's often because she has fielded many complaints from others. Or it's because he recognizes that the pastor is treading into dangerous territory, and so he is actually trying to protect the pastor from harm. In that case, the pastor may want to change the class or take more time to explain her thoughts better (don't preach about the evils of criticism no matter what the case is).

The point is that when we field a complaint, it is very important to know who the complainer is, despite the fact that the person relaying the complaint is trying to protect the complaining person. It's a delicate situation, so it's important to reassure the relayer that you will not divulge that you know who the complainer is. And you need to follow through by offering no recriminations or indication that you know who complained. In a similar way, it is important that church secretaries, office administrators, treasurers, program directors, and associate pastors don't automatically protect anonymity because doing so may actually create problems.

Ultimately, who does the complaining is more important than the complaint. Is the complainer a chip of ice, or the tip of an iceberg?

Proverb 10.

Criticism creates stagnation, but praise
stimulates creativity.

A LONG TIME AGO I SAW A SIGN in a store that I thought
was hilarious, so I had to buy it. It read, "The beatings will continue until morale improves." This sign
captures the issues inherent in so many churches that struggle.
Why do so many people think that criticism and denigration
will improve the situation? Too often churches are filled with
critical people who cynically criticize the pastor, the leaders,
the members, the ministry, the mission, and anything else going
on. Will angry criticisms really improve a pastor's preaching?
Will complaining that no one wants to do anything really get
them to do anything?

It is quite natural to criticize others. We get frustrated by
what others do or don't do, what organizations do or don't
do, and what groups do or don't do. So in our powerlessness
to effect change, we disparage or denigrate. Yet our denounce-
ments rarely effect long-lasting, positive change. For the most
part they foster stagnation. The more people criticize each
other, the more their criticism paralyzes others. Look at politics: does unending criticism really get people to work together
toward compromise?

Why do we criticize so much when it can gain so little?
There's an energy to criticism that captures people. You've
experienced it when you've been complaining about someone
or something, and it's like a demonic dynamo takes over you,
causing you to get angrier, louder, more passionate, and more
forceful. It feels good to be righteously indignant. It gets our
hearts stirring, our blood pumping, and it focuses our minds.
But it also creates a kind of torpor in others. When people go

into a critical rant, their ranting shuts us down as we just listen without responding. That's part of the problem with persistent criticism: *it shuts people down.*

Criticism is at the heart of dysfunction. Most people misunderstand dysfunction, thinking it means that things no longer function. That's not dysfunction, that's non-function. Dysfunction is *functioning in pain.* We function, but all of our efforts with others become painful as relationships break down. Persistently cynical criticism eventually creates dysfunction. And too often Christians are dysfunctional. It's what led someone to say, "Christianity is the only religion where people eat their own." I don't agree that it's the *only* religion, since Islam and Judaism seem to do a bit of eating of their own, too, but the point is still good. We Christians can be guilty of criticizing each other to death.

If we want to thrive and be creative, it requires an environment of praise. I don't mean empty praises or praise for praise's sake. I mean authentic praise when people accomplish things. I also mean an environment where people are appreciated and complimented for what they are doing rather than criticized for what they aren't doing. That doesn't mean that every accomplishment has to be celebrated publicly and lavishly. But it does mean that good things should be acknowledged in at least small words of appreciation because small praises spawn creativity.

So, if you want a congregation to become more hospitable, don't criticize them for their inhospitality, praise them for the small steps of hospitality they take. If you praise them, you'll create a "self-fulfilling prophecy" that helps them to be more hospitable. If you criticize them, you also create a self-fulfilling prophecy that leads them to become what you say they are—inhospitable. If you want people to give more, praise them for the generosity they have, rather than lambasting them for failing to give enough. If you want ministries to thrive, praise the good that is already taking place. If you want mission to thrive, praise people for taking small steps and engaging in small missions, which then helps prepare the way for them to take greater steps and engage in greater missions.

The key is to look for what's right rather than what's wrong, and to look for what's possible rather than what seems impossible.

Proverb 11.

Even if we will only lead a church for three years,
lead as though we will be there for thirty.

M OST PASTORS, when they start their ministry at a church, are eager to make a difference and to lead the church into the future. They come remembering what they were told in their church interviews: "We're ready for change. We want to change. And we want you to lead that change!" So the pastor takes them at their word and starts instituting changes. At first the changes seem to go okay, but soon there's a backlash. The congregation doesn't like the changes. They resist. And the same leaders who advocated change now don't back the pastor. They do nothing as conflict ensues. Wait! Didn't they say they were ready for change? Feelings get hurt. The pastor spends countless hours wondering what happened. Why was she or he was lied to? They said they wanted change, but really they just wanted to stay the same.

Actually, the pastor is wrong. They *did* want change. They just didn't want it at what feels to them like such a torrid pace—the pace at which the pastor is leading change. Most pastors suffer from what Chip and Dan Heath, in their book, *Made to Stick*,[1] call "the curse of knowledge." We are cursed by knowledge when we get so much training that we no longer remember what it was like not to know what we didn't know.

Pastors go to seminary to learn about how to lead change in a church (well, they go to learn about Bible, theology, and

_____

1. Chip Heath and Dan Heath, *Made to Stick: Why Some Ideas Survive and Others Die* (New York: Random House, 2007).

preaching, and hopefully get some instruction on church leadership along the way). They go to conferences on church transformation. They read books on leadership and church renewal. They take part in discussion groups on reforming the church. And in the process their knowledge curses them. They no longer remember what it was like before they had their knowledge, nor are they sensitive to the fact that no one in their congregation attended those conferences or read those books. Those creative strategies for church transformation, which seemed so simple to the pastor, are not so simple to the congregation. The pastor is cursed and doesn't know it. She or he no longer remembers what it was like not to know.

Leading a church toward transformation and renewal means that we pastors have to recognize that what seems like "one small step" for us is "a giant leap" for all church-kind. How do we overcome our curse in order to shower blessing? By understanding that even if we only plan to be in a congregation for three years, we need to lead them as though we will be there for thirty. That means taking our time. If we plan to be somewhere for thirty years, our perspective on change changes. We are willing to take our time.

Think of the process of church transformation like renovating a house. If we have to gut and transform the house in one year, the process will be incredibly messy, stressful, and filled with conflict. Lots of critical mistakes will be made, and a lot of the original work will have to be repaired later. The process and product will both be sloppy. But if we are willing to engage in that same process over many years, it can be done carefully in ways that lead to greater craftsmanship and long-lasting beauty. We take it one room at a time, which allows us to live in that space and more deeply appreciate each transformation.

Too many pastors are in too much of a hurry to build their legacy. They want quick transformation because they want their accomplishments to look good in the next interview for their next church. Or they are in a hurry to accomplish something that enables them to label their ministry a success. We are very cultural in that way. We want to be successful, and success is measured by tangible accomplishments.

The reality is that most of us are pastoring in churches that had their heyday a while ago. While we are responsible for at least making a valiant attempt to help them enter a new heyday, transformation still takes time, just as the church's decline took time. As a prominent researcher said about church growth, "If you want a church to really grow, start a new church. Transforming traditional churches is incredibly hard and takes time." He was right, but it can be done. We just have to be willing to take the time to craft that transformation.

So even if you only plan to be in the church for three years, pastor as though you will be there for thirty.

Proverb 12.

If a church won't say to God, "Thy will be done,"
then God will let their will be done, even if
it leads to their demise.

THIS IS A TRICKY PROVERB because it all hinges on whether the members, leaders, and pastors of a church truly want to seek God's will for their church. In other words, are they willing to discern prayerfully what God is seeking, or are they satisfied seeking their own will, the majority's will, or the pastor's will? Just because a church acts like it wants to do God's will doesn't mean they actively seek it.

The truth is that in most of our churches, prayerfully seeking God's will is an afterthought—or maybe not a thought at all. We're pretty good at following *Robert's Rules of Order*. We're pretty good at following the meeting and decision-making processes used by the local school board, the township board, and the company board. But we're not particularly good at following the model of Acts, where the apostles gather, pray, sometimes fast, and seek God's guidance (see Acts 1:21–26 and 13:1–3).

In other words, the apostles genuinely asked, "God, what is your will?" And then they listened and followed in faith, saying, "Thy will be done." This isn't exactly the model we follow. We tend to seek some combination of what we want, what the pastor wants, what the members want, and then ask God to bless our will. We say to God, "My will be done."

When deciding whether or not to start a Vacation Bible School the following summer, do we ask whether or not we are being led in that direction by God? If we are entering into a new mission initiative, do we pray over it first to discern whether or not we are called into that initiative? Just because a mission is a good idea, and might be something we "should" do, doesn't mean that it is what we are called to do.

Most churches sincerely do want to serve God, but that doesn't mean that they are asking God how God wants them to serve. Instead, they make their choices rationally, procedurally, and corporately. That may work in business, but does that really have us asking, "God, what is your will?"

When churches don't ask prayerfully, "God, what is your will?" God then responds by letting them suffer the consequences of doing only their own will. True discernment is hard. It requires people of faith coming together and prayerfully listening for a sense of God's will in a process filled with ambiguity.

In the end, churches that won't pray and say to God, "Thy will be done," end up having God say to them, "Okay, then thy will be done." Is it any wonder they decline?

Proverb 13.

The difference between God being nowhere and God
being now here is the space we create for God.

BUSYNESS PLAGUES NORTH AMERICAN LIFE. We value busyness. We prize full schedules. We wear our 24/7, 365 as a badge of honor. We might wish wistfully that we could go to a deserted island to get some rest, but we'd most likely choose the deserted island with wifi so we could take our smartphones. Is it any wonder that so many people question whether God is really here? Is it any wonder that so many people now confidently proclaim that God is nowhere?

No one can get a sense of God's presence without creating space for God's presence. The pace of modern life dulls our inner awareness of God. Just as the parent who is busy doing five tasks at once often can't hear her child in the background shouting, "Mom! Mom! Mom!" we have a hard time hearing God whispering our name because of the many things that cry for our attention.

On a personal level this is tragic, but the modern striving of so many churches is to become like the culture. Successful churches are considered to be the ones that seem the busiest. They're the ones that have a thousand programs going on at the same time. They're the ones that seem to be engaged in all sorts of mission. We measure the success of a church by how much ministry is going on, how many people show up for worship, how many members the church has, and how many missionaries it sends out. We measure a church by its quantities: how much does it have going on? It's good to have an active church, but is our activity the true measure of God's presence?

The problem is that the more a church strives to do, the more it can actually obscure God. This is not a plea for a church to do nothing. It's recognizing that when a church measures itself by its busyness, it also can create the conditions for people to experience God as *nowhere*. The members can become so busy doing God's work that they no longer experience God. They lack the space to experience God.

The Christian mystical tradition—the deeper spiritual tradition that much of the modern church both ignores and dismisses—is a tradition of creating space for God. It is a tradition rooted in prayer, contemplation, creating time and space to get a sense that God is *now here*. In the church world, it is a tradition that seeks what God wants over what we want; that invites leaders to learn how to pray and to discern; that doesn't just try to placate people or stimulate them, but that tries to deepen them to discover that God is now here.

There's a balance to be kept in our churches between being active for God and being receptive to God; between serving God and opening to God; between busyness and prayerfulness. In the modern trend toward increased mission, we can forget the fact that if mission doesn't begin in prayer and discernment, it can end up as an attempt to just get busy for God. It creates the conditions where we push God to the margins and treat God as though God is nowhere. If we are to live out the idea that God is now here, we have to create space to ask first, "Is this really my calling? Is this really our calling? If so, how are we called to act on it?" And if that isn't done in prayer, both individually and communally, it doesn't get done at all.

The difference between God being nowhere and God being now here is the space we create for God to guide us to our calling.

Proverb 14.

Church, as well as faith, is about relationships, not rightness or righteousness, because in the end true righteousness comes from right relationships.

TOO MANY CHRISTIANS, TOO MANY CHURCHES, and too many ministries and missions pursue rightness and righteousness over relationships, and it is a reason our churches struggle today.

We all want to be right, and we all want to be righteous, but how right and righteous can we actually be? I love a quote from C. S. Lewis's book, *The Great Divorce*, that deals with what we learn in heaven after we die: "That's what we all find when we reach [heaven]. We've all been wrong! That's the great joke. There's no need to go on pretending one was right! After that we begin living."[1]

After that we begin living. Too many people live their lives trying to be right, and they never recognize that their pursuits ultimately make them wrong. It doesn't matter what they want to be right about. It may be about politics, as they fight about the rightness of the right or the righteousness of the left. It may be about their theological positions. It may be about their sports teams. It may be about what money should be spent on this or that program. Or it may be as simple as who was responsible for taking the dog for a walk. We all have a need to be right, and we all feel a deficit of "rightness." And we spend much of our day wanting to be right somehow, someway, even if it's only in the smallest victory—"I was right! Blueberries really are purple, not blue!"

---

1. C. S. Lewis, *The Great Divorce* (New York: MacMillan Publishing Company, 1946): 95.

We are just as wrong when it comes to pursuing righteousness. We all want to be righteous in God's eyes, and we all tend to get a little self-righteous at times. It's amazing how often Christians are convinced of their own righteousness, and of someone else's wronged-ness. How rare it is to find someone willing to promote someone else's righteousness and their own unrighteousness.

Despite the arguments to the contrary, real rightness and righteousness come from relationships. Righteousness comes from love—love of God, love of others, love of self. If we cannot love, we cannot live in God's righteousness because the crux of the Gospel is loving the Lord our God with all our heart, mind, soul, and strength, and others as ourselves. Righteousness comes out of our being made "right" through our relationship with Christ, and that only comes through our loving God enough to allow God's love to transform and work through us. And that's true, whether we are talking about a church or a person.

Too many churches see attendance, membership, and programs as the measurement of success—how many are here, how many belong to here, and how many groups and activities are produced here. The real measurement of success is how much we care for others. The former is a measurement of how right we must be because we look successful. The latter is a measurement of how much we love and embody our relationships with God, others, and self.

When it comes to creating healthy congregations, they can only be created when a church puts relationships above all else—relationships with God, others, and ourselves. Churches that seek righteousness eventually end up in divisiveness. Pastors who seek rightness and righteousness generally become overly self-righteous, ruling over their little dysfunctional kingdoms. They claim that they are leading the righteous to God, but in the end they lead them down selfishly sinful paths.

There are many forms of self-righteousness. There can be the pastor or person who moralizes constantly, trying to cram an ever-shrinking halo around her or his ever-expanding head. Or there can be the pastor or person striving for justice, who self-righteously demands that we care about the oppressed, while simultaneously oppressing those who can't seem to catch their vision. They become so certain that they are right that their ends always justify their means, their sinfulness always masquerades as saintliness, and their self-righteousness obliterates their relationships.

In the end, congregational life is about forming a relational life together. What matters is our relationships with God and others. If ministry or mission cause us to become dysfunctional because they become more important than the people involved in them, we need to cut them off and fling them away. If our sermons are causing divisiveness, we need to learn to let our sermons serve God, not try to force God to serve our sermons.

Ultimately we need to seek relationships rather than righteousness and rightness because in the end those loving relationships lead us to righteousness and rightness—righteousness because we now have a right relationship with God, and rightness because all we seek is God's love and grace, which makes everything right.

Proverb 15.

*In life and ministry, we can't get others to care
about us by trying to get others to care about us.
We only get others to care about us when we spend
our lives caring about others.*

TOO OFTEN OUR CHURCHES ARE FILLED with people who want others to care about them more than they want to care about others. This reality is one of the biggest problems in life and ministry: too many of us spend our lives trying to get others to care about us, and we are continually disappointed with the results. We use lots of strategies to get people to care about us. Some of us are more narcissistic, and we can never get enough of other people's adulation, attention, and admiration. Others see ourselves as victims, and we hope others will care about us because we are long-suffering, sad, objects of sympathy. Still others of us have a hard time fitting in, and we obsess about how others neglect, negate, or take no notice of us.

In all of these cases we never get people to care about us because our gaze is on ourselves, not on others, and when we gaze too intently on ourselves we never notice the needs of others. The deep Christian life is a life lived for others, and the ministers and ministries that grasp this end up forming relationships in which they both care and feel cared about.

A number of years ago I gave a talk in which one of the pastors attending complained of feeling lonely and as though no one in her congregation cared about her. Whether you agree or disagree with my response, I told her that God put her in a leadership role to care about others, not to be cared about. As long as her focus was her loneliness and the lack of care, the members of her church wouldn't care about her because she wasn't really caring about them. They called her to be the person who leads them to care, who teaches them how to care. It was only in leading them to care by caring about them that she would eventually find them caring about her.

Her ministry and church were very much like many of our churches. They are filled with people whose main focus is being cared about. They want pastors to be their chaplains, and they want their churches to be sanatoriums where people convalesce from the pains of life. And this is why these churches stagnate. The churches and ministries that are vibrant are the ones that want their pastors to be leaders not chaplains, leading them to love others. They also want their churches to be centers for servants, not sanatoriums for the selfish.

Churches that have the greatest sense of love are those that know they are a church for others. As a result, they actually enhance their ability to be loved by others. In churches that have a great love for others, that love ends up returning back to them. But churches with a great love for self end up losing that love.

The woman who taught me this most deeply was named Jo. I visited her weeks before her death from brain cancer. She did not remember who I was, but remembered that I was someone important to her. She couldn't speak, but when I visited her she took my hands, poured lotion on them, and rubbed the lotion in my hands. I was there to visit her, but all she wanted to do was to care for me. She was one of the reasons our church had been a place of caring for years. Even when she was in great need of care, her focus was on caring for another. She made it easy for others to care for her because she had lived a life of caring for others.

Ministry literally means "servant-ry," and to be a place of ministry means to be a place of serving. We can't serve others if we constantly demand that others serve us.

Proverb 16.

*We are ultimately called to apostleship, not
discipleship. Discipleship is a stage on the way to
apostleship. To be a disciple is to be a student, but
to be an apostle is to be a sent servant.*

I N CHURCH CIRCLES, IT HAS BEEN POPULAR for a number
of years to say that we are called to "make disciples," and
that one of the main purposes of a church is "disciple
making." That makes a lot of sense, especially since Jesus says
that we are to "*Go therefore and make disciples of all nations,
baptizing them in the name of the Father and of the Son and
of the Holy Spirit, and teaching them to obey everything that I
have commanded you*" (Matthew 28:19–20a).

Far be it from me to suggest that we aren't called to make
people disciples of Christ. But is disciple making the end of
the journey? Is that really all that churches are called to do?

I think there's more. Most people don't think very deeply
about what it means to be a disciple. The word "disciple"
comes from the Latin word *discipuli*, which means "student."
Back when I was in seventh grade, our Latin teacher, Mrs.
Hutchinson, would walk into the room and shout out, "*Salve
discipuli!*" and we would respond, "*Salve magister!*" In other
words, "*Hello students!*" "*Hello teacher!*" Is Christ's main
focus really that we would just become students? I appreciate
the need to learn. I've been a student for a significant portion
of my life. But there's more to the life of faith than just learning about the life of faith.

Jesus's inner circle was made up of students—disciples
(*discipuli*)—before the crucifixion, but they didn't remain
disciples. After the resurrection they became *apostles*. They
became "sent ones," being sent out to serve God in the

world. Their discipleship was important, but it was always geared toward service. The disciples spent three years learning how to teach, preach, heal, serve, care, and love. And then they were sent out to teach, preach, heal, serve, care, and love, thus helping others grow in faith so that over time they could become "sent ones" who teach, preach, heal, serve, care, and love. Paul is the great example of this. After his conversion, he spent at least eleven years as a student, as a disciple, before he was called to become an apostle and reach out to the gentiles.

Many of our churches are satisfied just to teach. They are content to create disciples, as though that is an end in itself. They create all sorts of small groups, offer classes, and create programs, all to teach people how to live a Christian life. But learning isn't enough. We don't go to school just to go to school. We go to school to prepare ourselves for everything we face in life. Our culture values learning, but learning must have a purpose. If our purpose is merely to make disciples, then we are creating a class of perpetual religious students. While Jesus called on us to "make disciples of all nations," it was a calling to invite them all to learn about God, to grow in God, to become grounded in God, all so that we could learn to serve God.

Still, I don't want to dismiss the importance of discipleship. The discipleship phase is important. Sometimes there's a failure to recognize that mission and apostleship come with maturity and that formation is important along the way. We push mission as the salvation of the church, thinking that if we get people involved in reaching out, they will become healthier. The problem is that mission that isn't grounded in faith and prayerful seeking of God's will, ends up serving us, not God. And it leads people to become burned out because they aren't prepared to serve. So Christian service is built on Christian study. Mission naturally arises out of maturity, but only with those who are committed to learning to grow in

Christian maturity. In other words, discipleship nurtures apostleship, and apostleship can nurture greater apostleship, but first a person has to grow through discipleship.

Those of a deep Christian spirituality understand the connection between discipleship and apostleship. Too often I've heard those who don't understand Christian spirituality label Christian mystics and contemplatives as navel gazers. I've yet to meet a true contemplative who isn't also missional. Close contact and grounding in God always leads to service because that's what God calls us to. We can't grow in discernment without discerning God's call to serve in tangible, practical ways.

The life of mission requires a life of prayer, and that life of prayer is formed out of a commitment to becoming disciples. But the purpose is to serve and be sent.

Proverb 17.

When making a change in a church that people think is wrong, try it long enough to determine whether it is wrong because it's actually wrong or because it just feels wrong.

THE FACT IS THAT ALL CHURCHES RESIST CHANGE, or at least all churches that are old enough to no longer remember those who founded the church. In a changing world, many people want their churches to be the one place that offers consistency and stability. They want it to be the one place that never changes.

Unfortunately, a church that never changes—that never adapts to a changing world, that never adjusts to cultural shifts and new generations, and that never strives to do things better—ends up slowly dying. And when a church stops growing it starts dying.

The major issue is that people don't like change, so changes in worship will always be resisted, at least until people become used to the changes. That's really the question with change: people can't tell at first whether a change is wrong or just unfamiliar.

Too often church leaders confuse the two. They worry that because members don't like a change, it may be wrong. But quite often good changes need time to sink in. Giving a change time to sink in is important. Most changes in worship need at least two to three months of time before people can distinguish between what's wrong and what feels wrong.

In our own church, we've made many changes that were resisted at first and embraced later. We replaced the typically stodgy, responsive Call to Worship with a Taizé-style chant and time of quiet prayer. Many didn't like it at first because it wasn't what people were used to. Now members don't ever want to go back to the traditional Call to Worship because it feels mechanical and wooden, while the new opening feels centering and Spirit-filled. We've moved scripture to the beginning of worship so that people can discover how it is reflected in the hymns and written prayers. At first people didn't like it because that's not where the scripture is read in our denominational tradition. Now people appreciate it because they see how the scripture passage influences the whole service. We tried offering contemporary worship services for several months before people came to. . . . Actually, they never liked it even after several months. This led us to move in a different direction after we realized that contemporary worship was wrong for us, even if it is right for other churches. But we gave ourselves time to distinguish between what's unfamiliar and what's wrong.

Even the best of changes are resisted. Giving ourselves the time to distinguish between what is wrong and what just feels wrong helps us determine whether the change is best or just plain bad.

Proverb 18.

When trying to determine whether to engage in a new ministry or mission, focus on "what are we called to do" rather than "what should we do."

CHURCHES CONSISTENTLY FIND WAYS to push God to the margins. They don't mean to. They may not necessarily want to (although I do suspect that many Christians fear direct contact with God). They do it without realizing it by focusing on what they should do rather than what they are called to do.

"Should" is a powerful word in ministry or mission. As Christians and as churches, we are called to reach out and make a difference in the world. We want to make a difference in the world. And there is no shortage of deep needs we can address in the world. The problem is that there is also no shortage of people who are happy to tell us what in the world we should do: "We should start a ministry to provide coats to the homeless." "We should offer parenting classes for our young parents." "We should start a Saturday night service to reach out to those who can't come on Sunday." "We should create an afterschool program." "We should offer meditation classes."

All of these are great ideas and would make wonderful ministries and missions. All would be good for a church to do. The question, though, isn't whether we *should* do them. The question is whether we are *called* to do them. The difference between the two is ginormous.

"Shoulds" are grounded in external pressures that arise out of the need to justify ourselves, appear relevant, follow trends, and/or diminish grumbling. We say we should do something because we feel guilty not doing it; we feel irrelevant when others do it and we don't; we feel frustrated that no one else is doing it; or we hear people complaining about the problem, and we feel we need to do something to get people to stop.

The reality is that probably someone "should" do something about all of these issues. But that's not the same as saying that *we* are "called" to do something about them. There were a lot of "shoulds" that Jesus never did. Perhaps he "should" have done something about the problem of slavery. Maybe he "should" have done more about the problem of rampant divorce in his times. Possibly he "should" have done more about breaking the Roman oppression of the Jewish people. In fact, there is much scholarly speculation that Judas betrayed Jesus because he thought Jesus "should" be a military messiah ushering in a new age of Jewish power. He thought Jesus "should" call on an army of angels to smite the Roman Empire. By betraying him he thought he could force Jesus's hand and get him to do what many thought the messiah would do: usher in a new age by divine force. The problem was that Judas was a "should" kind of guy, while Jesus responded only to his calling. Calling forth an army of angels was not his call.

Look at the root of virtually all that Jesus did and you will see a man of prayer who sought only the Father's call. He went into the desert because the Spirit called him to go there. He preached, taught, and healed in response to the Father's call. He went to the cross because the Father called him to do so. Throughout his ministry, Jesus spent a tremendous amount of time in prayer seeking God's call. His ministry and mission were rooted in calls, not shoulds. And the early church was rooted in calls, not shoulds.

In doing ministry and mission, the primary question can't be "Should we do this?" Instead, ministry and mission need to be rooted in a prayerful asking, "Is God calling us to do this?" The change in question makes all the difference in the world. Asking if we are called to do something roots our ministry or mission in God's will. Asking if we should do something roots us in human will.

When we respond merely to a "should," success is based on our energies and efforts. When we respond to a call, success is based on the Spirit's presence and power. In other words, when we do what we should, we only accomplish what *we could*. But when we do what we are called, we accomplish what *God can*.

Proverb 19.

*Treat all people as though they are forgiven people,
not sinful people, because that's what they are.*

ONE OF THE SAD FACTS ABOUT CHURCH LIFE is that
we so often treat others as though they are sinful
through and through. Christianity may be a faith
that recognizes the sinfulness of people, but it never, ever
advocates treating people as though they are sinful.

Christian faith cherishes the power of love over the emphasis on sin. It is a faith that attempts to transform through love
rather than through criticism, judgment, and attack. Notice
how often Jesus criticizes others for being sinful, and com-
pare that to the approach of the Pharisees, the Sadducees, and
the scribes. He rarely calls anyone sinful. They constantly do.
In fact, Jesus's main criticism of those three groups is their
lack of love toward those immersed in sin, and their sinfulness
because of their lack of love. They have a love of law. Jesus
has a law of love.

Notice that Jesus only rarely focused his ministry on the
righteous. He focused his ministry on the sinful, but rather
than criticizing them, he loved them. Jesus continually reached
out in love to the prostitute, the Samaritan woman by the
well, the Centurion and his servant, the tax collectors, the
Syrophoenician woman, the Canaanite woman, the woman
with the twelve-year hemorrhage, and so many more. They
might have been sinful, but he responded with love by forgiv-
ing and healing them.

But, but, but . . . didn't he tell them to go and sin no
more? Yes, once, to the woman caught in adultery. He also
said, "your sins are forgiven" twice: once to the paralytic
lowered through the roof (well, three times, but it is the

same story in Matthew, Mark, and Luke), and once to the sinful woman who anointed him and wiped his feet with her tears.

In other words, Jesus led with love. And that's how we need to be in our churches, especially as pastors and leaders. Too many pastors see the members of a church either as a help or a hindrance to their personal goals. They lead with their ambitions. They want the church to grow in membership, mission, giving, or some other number, and they see their members as either supporting or subverting those goals. In other words, they lead with something other than love. And when the members fail to deliver their help or support, they are then treated as though they are sinful. Too many ministries falter over the tendency to see others as sinful.

As leaders in a church, we need to treat everyone as though they are forgiven, because they are. This is one of the most essential keys to church growth of any kind: if we love the people of the church, and if we let them know that we love them, the church will grow missionally, numerically, and in generosity. The reason is that our love for them will allow their love to grow and to spread. On the other hand, if we see them and treat them as though they are sinful, then the church will wither because people will act out of their sin, not their love.

Treat everyone as though she or he is forgiven and loved. It will be like spring rain after a winter thaw.

Proverb 20.

When you love and praise people, you help them grow. When you criticize them, you make them wither. When you love and praise churches, you help them grow. When you criticize them, you make them wither.

YEARS AGO I POSTED A SIGN in our offices that said, *"The Beatings Will Continue until Morale Improves"* (I mentioned this in Proverb 10). I loved that sign because it spoke the truth in its absurdity. No one would ever believe that beatings could lead to improved morale, but a lot of people think their constant criticisms will somehow improve behavior, performance, and relationships.

Sometimes criticism is necessary, but it is like radiation. In small doses it gets rid of something toxic, but in large doses it kills.

Criticism can motivate people in the short term, but in the long term it kills their motivation. Years ago there was a National Hockey League coach who excelled at using criticism for motivation. He managed to take three separate teams to the championship series, eventually winning on his third try. But he was almost always fired or had to abruptly resign midway through the following season because the players would no longer play for him. He got them to win through insults, public belittling, personal mocking, and mind games. It worked for a while because the players hated him so much that they would do anything to get him off their backs. But eventually they stopped playing hard. They became lethargic and sloppy. His criticism eventually caused them to wither as a team.

Perhaps you're thinking, "But he won championships!" Yes, but he lost life! He lost people. He killed relationships. He missed what really mattered. We can possibly get short-term gains through criticism, but what church seeks only short-term gains? Ministry is a long-term endeavor. Yet so many church leaders think that criticism can eventually lead to growth. Pastors criticize members in sermons, in meetings, and in private. Members criticize pastors and other members through snide comments, gossip, and sometimes public beratings. Both use sarcasm and cynicism to get their way in the short term, but they lead the church to wither in the long term as members stop volunteering, serving, and at some point showing up.

People eventually become how we treat them to be. If we treat them as failures, they will fail. If we treat them as beloved, they will love. Churches are no different. When leaders treat them as failures, they fail. But when leaders love them, they become loving.

So many church leaders act as though they believe that criticism will grow a church, but it won't. It doesn't help churches, children, pets, plants, or anything else thrive—or at least not for long. Think about it this way: Most people in therapy are trying to recover from long-term criticism. Good therapists help them recover what is good. Who would ever go to a therapist who does nothing but criticize?

Loving others, praising others, finding what is good in others is fundamental to growing churches and ministries. People, pets, plants, and churches thrive when they are loved and praised. I don't mean false praises, but real praises that demonstrate love. If our church is struggling to thrive, or even survive, turn on the love and learn to praise. This is Jesus's secret. He met sinners and found what was good in them, especially when they had lived life amidst insults, criticisms, neglect, and abuse. His criticisms were always reserved for people who excelled at criticizing, belittling, judging, and ostracizing others.

If you love and praise your church, it will begin to thrive. If you love and praise those around you, they will thrive. Otherwise, they will eventually wither.

Proverb 21.

Church life requires balance, and when there is
no balance in the church, the people fall.

WE LIVE IN A TIME WHEN PEOPLE worship activity. They throw around phrases like "available 24/7!" wearing the designation as a badge of honor. The attributes we praise in people are how hard they work, how available they are, and how little personal life they have. In fact, I've noticed that on television most crime dramas involve single characters who seem to work 24 hours a day. Are they the model for the modern agnostic monk? They're devoted to work, follow a creed, commit themselves to service, and seem to live celibate lives, yet express little interest in God or religion.

What does being available 24/7 gain us? We are slaves to our mobile phones and all they contain—calls, text messages, emails, voicemails, and apps. And this kind of life has infected the church. We measure a church's success by how many activities it has. What does a church offer the children in terms of education, activities, and entertainment? What does the church offer in terms of small groups and educational opportunities? How many ministries can the church list on its website? How many show up for worship and are listed on the membership rolls? In fact, the churches we deem the most successful are the ones that have the most activity, are the most fully embracing of social media and technology, and that seem to be available for anything 24/7. They may be active, but are they balanced?

Churches often contribute to the lack of balance we see in our culture. We are an out-of-balance culture, and our churches strive to imitate this imbalance. In the talks I've given, I've often run a short exercise to see how well people recognize the balance between ministry and prayer in the gospels. I'll ask people to think about the gospels and reflect on how active Jesus was. They notice him constantly traveling to preach, teach, and heal. What they don't notice is how often he goes off to pray, refresh, and restore himself.

Before launching his ministry, he spends forty days fasting and praying in the desert. He constantly goes off to a mountain, a lonely place, or a garden to pray. He is the epitome of balance. His prayer life supports his ministry, and his ministry is a response to his prayer life. He is balanced.

We aren't balanced like Jesus, no matter how much we might want to imitate him. A significant number of our church members teeter constantly on the edge of burnout. And our churches don't help. We constantly look to how we can get our members engaged, but not necessarily to how we can deepen their prayer lives and help them mature spiritually. Just because someone is active doesn't mean that she or he is growing deeper in faith and maturity. In fact, one of the reasons churches struggle to get people engaged has to do with this lack of balance.

Do you know about the 80/20 rule? It's the lament in churches that twenty percent of the members do eighty percent of the work. Do you know why this occurs? It's not that the eighty percent don't want to do the work. It's that the twenty percent are often so unbalanced in their lives that they overextend themselves in ministry and don't leave any room for the eighty percent to be involved. I've often thought that the problem with having such active churches, or at least such active people within the churches, is that we contribute to their lack of balance between church and life. I see my role as a pastor to be as much about inviting people to let go of ministries as it is to invite people to be part of ministries.

Churches often create imbalance, rather than offering balance. When I first started as pastor of my church, I noticed that our elders not only attended our board meetings, but they also were asked to chair committees, visit members, serve as ushers, count money after worship once a month, and serve communion once a month. My first act was to get them to let go of everything except attending the board meetings and chairing a committee. A few complained that no one would step up to do the rest. I responded that no one would step up till they stepped down. Since then we've created a fairly strong visitation team, a rotation of six teams of ushers, a rotation of four teams of communion servers, and a number of other people to do other parts of ministry. And we don't burn people out.

When a church becomes unbalanced, people eventually fall. We have to find ways to create more balance between activity and prayer, between sharing ministry and mission, and between church and life.

Proverb 22.

*Don't become so theologically pure in your ministry
that it becomes spiritually foolish.*

W E IN THE PROTESTANT TRADITION love our theology. We love to think about big things: the nature of the Trinity, the meaning of the cross and resurrection, the purpose of creation, the divinity and humanity of Christ, and terms such as salvation, sanctification, atonement, perichoresis, the delay of the parousia, and many, many more. A good number of pastors were originally attracted to ministry because they yearned to learn and preach theology.

The danger of falling in love with theology, especially in our approach to church leadership, is that we can become so heady that we lose people's hearts. We can strive so much for orthodoxy (whether of a conservative or liberal kind) that we ignore people's spirits. For example, I recently heard a pastor say that God has created other religions to winnow the wheat from the chaff. In other words, God created other faiths because God doesn't want to save everyone, but only a certain remnant. So God created other religions to siphon people away from Christ, allowing God to reduce the number who are saved. That's a foolish theology. It's disconnected spiritually, and it kills faith in a church. It teaches that the God of love doesn't really love as much as we thought. Worse, it portrays God as being judgmental, capricious, and arbitrary, which has the unintended consequence of driving people away from God, church, and pastors. Why pursue God when God may consider you chaff?

For a church to really help connect people with God, it needs a theology grounded in Christian spirituality—one with a vibrant connection with God. That does not mean that our spirituality won't have a theological foundation. I see spirituality as the breath of faith, but theology is the bones of faith, and religious practice is the body of faith. Get rid of any one of them and you either have a blob (no bones), wind rattling bones (no practice), or a corpse (no breath). Theology gives structure to our spirituality, but it is still thinking *about* God, not necessarily a connection *with* God.

Our preaching, teaching, and theological thinking must be grounded in leading people to encounter, experience, and embrace God. If our theology becomes so speculative that it has no connection to our relationship with Christ, and no personal awareness of the Spirit, it becomes meaningless to most people. We have that problem already with the Trinity. We talk so much about the relationship between the three persons of God that we lose touch with the more important, intimate, personal relationships between us and the Creator, Christ, and Holy Spirit.

To be in leadership in a church, and especially to be a pastor, doesn't mean to be merely the theologian-in-residence. Why? Because Jesus was never merely a theologian-in-residence. Jesus was the teacher-in-residence, the preacher-in-residence, the healer-in-residence, the prayer-in-residence, the presence-of-God-in-residence, and the savior-in-residence. He didn't just preach theology. He actually cared for the whole being: spirit, mind, and body.

In leading a church, we have to temper our theology with a pragmatic and real-life spirituality. To cut out the spiritual in favor of mere theologizing means to become foolish as we cut out the connection with God. A theology that opens people spiritually opens the church to life.

Proverb 23.

You can't do anything about things you can't do anything about, but you can do things about things you can do something about. So focus on what you can do something about, and let go of what you can't do anything about.

THE BIGGEST TRAP FOR ANY PASTOR or church leader is obsessing about things we can't do anything about. Why? Because once you start digging into what's persistently wrong, you eventually end up in a pit of despair.

We can't change the fact that our churches have gotten old. We can't do anything about the fact that popular culture is so disdainful of church, Christianity, and religion. We can't do anything about the fact that we inhabit old buildings, while the seemingly successful, growing churches have new, high-tech buildings. We can't generally control the bad behavior of our members, and especially of our lay leaders (or pastors, sadly). We can't control who does or doesn't show up on Sunday mornings. We can obsess about these things, but we can't control them. And runaway obsessions can eventually lead to depression.

Unfortunately, far too many pastors focus their attention on things they have no control over. As a spiritual director and mentor, I get the opportunity to talk to a lot of pastors, and I'm convinced that a huge number of our mainline church pastors live in secret depression. It may not be a depression that requires medication, but it is a situational depression that grows out of being consumed by what's wrong with their churches.

We pastors struggle over things that are out of our control: The members don't sing loudly enough. They seldom or insincerely compliment us on our sermons. They don't always show up for meetings. They always sit in the same pew. We can feel so underappreciated and unrequited that it slowly degrades our passion for ministry. What we don't realize is that focusing on what we can't change is sapping our energy for what we can change. Think Jesus obsessed about what he couldn't change? I think he focused on what he could change, and he let God and the passage of time take care of the rest.

In our church we've had a number of seminary interns. Eventually each one complained to me about how hard it is to preach in our early worship service because the members worshiped with a lower energy than our second service. They loved our second service because it had energy. I've always taught them that they can't control the energy they get from a congregation, but they can control the energy they give to the congregation. So if a congregation isn't giving them enough energy, then summon up more energy of their own and give it to the congregation. In other words, don't outsource our spirits. Instead, tap into the Spirit within. We can't control the congregation's energy, but we can control ours.

Focusing on what we can do is a key to doing well in ministry. Too many church consultants teach churches to shore up their weaknesses. My suggestion is to build on their strengths. A church may not be able to create a vibrant small-group ministry, but they may be able to build a strong dinner ministry. They may not be able to do a mission to Africa, but they may be able to do a mission to the food bank. They may not have great music in worship, but they might be led to have great spirit in worship.

Focusing on what we can do something about is really important. But even more important is learning to tell the difference between what we can and can't do. It isn't worth our time wallowing in self-pity and sadness over what isn't there. Let it go and wallow in recognition and gladness over what is there. And then look at how you can build on it.

Proverb 24.

If you've bitten off more than you can chew as a church, spit it out and take smaller bites. You don't have to do everything all at once.

ONE OF THE FAMILY STORIES WE LOVE to laugh about is the "Olive Story." When my daughter was young, she loved black olives. She can't stand them now, but back then they were one of her favorite foods. She loved to place the olives on the tips of her fingers, and then hold up her hand as she wiggled her olive-capped fingers. One-by-one she popped an olive-full finger into her mouth, and then pulled back her olive-less finger to show us.

At the Olive Garden one night, she ordered a small plate of olives. But she was too full to eat them by the end of the meal. So we told the waitress to take them as she cleared the plates. Suddenly, our daughter grabbed all of the olives and hastily stuffed them into her mouth. She crammed in at least twelve. We stared in surprise at the bulging-cheeked five year old with black goo seeping out of her mouth. I said to her, "Sweetie-pie, you didn't have to eat them all right now. If you didn't want her to take them away, all you had to do was to say so. Spit them out and we'll get you new olives." So she spit out the disgusting black mess back onto the plate as we all laughed (including her).

So much of the pressure of modern church life reminds me of the Olive Story. With the rise of megachurches there has also emerged an intense pressure to be seen as relevant by doing as much as possible. We measure our success as pastors, leaders, and churches by how much we are doing. The problem is that when we try to do too much, we end up with a gooey mess.

God doesn't expect us to do everything as a church. That's the reason why there are so many churches. Whether we accept all the other churches as being part of the same body of Christ as us, we are indeed all part of Christ's body. Whether it's the large megachurch that has hundreds of programs, or the small church that mainly worships, provides food for a local food cupboard, gives money to several mission ventures, and has Sunday School for five children—all are part of Christ's body.

What matters isn't how much we do, but the extent to which we do what we do with care. Looking at the Bible, the original churches weren't measured by how active they were. They were measured by the extent to which they had a passionate love for God and others. We continually measure our modern churches using the metrics of our modern culture. We think that large numbers equal success. But as many have noted, those large megachurches can be a mile wide and an inch deep.

The key is that we need to learn to take smaller bites of ministry and mission, and then let them slowly build up into something greater. Take our time digesting what God is calling us to do, and then move on to the next one.

Ultimately, trying to do too much as leaders leads people to become burned out. Burnout is the result of too much that leads to too little—too much pressure, too much expectation, and too much to do, coupled with too little time to think things through, too little ability to prepare, and too little reward. All of these are the result of biting off more than we can chew.

A key to successful ministry and mission is understanding what the right amount is, and only digesting what we can chew . . . and do.

Proverb 25.

Discernment means trusting in a plan that God never fully reveals and that we never fully understand, but trusting God to take care of it all in the end anyway.

O NE OF THE MOST IMPORTANT THINGS we can do as Christians, and even more as congregations, is to prayerfully seek God's will when making decisions. This is the biblical model. It's the Gospel model. It's the Jesus model.

Did you know that there was an ancient reason why Jesus went into the desert for forty days before starting his ministry? He was following in the footsteps of Adam and Eve, Abraham, Israel, Moses, the Israelites out of Egypt, David, Elijah, and the Israelites in exile. The desert was the place to most deeply discover God's will. Discerning what God wants requires space and time, with few distractions and lots of silence. The Holy Spirit led Jesus into the desert so that he could build his mission on a foundation of prayerful seeking and doing. Without a foundation of listening for divine guidance amidst temptation, his ministry would crumble.

The problem for most Christians today is that they don't really seek God's will, whether that's as individuals or as congregations. Yes, people read the Bible to try to figure out what God wants. Yes, people pray for God's guidance. What they don't do is follow Jesus's example of seeking the quiet of the desert, and of the mountain, path, or garden.

The desert is a powerful place to hear God because it forces people to give up their desires, pride and ego, ambitions, achievements, and power. There is no power in the desert—only the powerlessness of a solitary prayer: *God, what do you want from and for me?* How often do we ask this question sincerely and passionately, whether as individuals or congregations? We don't typically ask in honest prayer what God wants from and for us. Instead, we try to get God to confirm what we already want to do. Or we try to convince God to bless and make great what we already plan to do. Really seeking what God wants means letting go of what we want, and who wants to do that?

Jesus sought the Father's will throughout his ministry and mission by spending time in the desert, on the mountain, in lonely places, and especially in the Garden of Gethsemane. The apostles were constantly seeking God's will in prayer—prayer that led to visions, inspirations, and insight. And they were passionate both about laying aside what they wanted and seeking what God wanted.

Needing to lay aside what we want for what God wants reveals the fundamental problem with discernment: *When we try to discern God's will, we never really know what God's will is.* We get a sense of it, we get glimpses of it, we see the possibility of it, but it's never enough to erase our uncertainties, doubts, and pragmatic concerns. What if what we sense is wrong? What if we follow and God abandons us? What if it doesn't work?

It's these uncertainties, doubts, and concerns that prompt many of us to quit discerning and start deciding for ourselves—albeit in a discernment-seeming way. We pore over the Bible for clear scriptural proof, but it ends up being proof that confirms what we already believed and wanted. We cite our carefully thought out theological formulations to rationally justify our previously chosen courses of action. We substitute our rigid ideologies for God's voice, believing that God is already behind our theological beliefs, our political affiliations, and our moral stands—whether or not God really is. As a result, we vote on congregational issues by asking, *"All in favor say 'yes,'"* rather than encouraging people to spend time in quiet and vote, asking, *"All who sensed in prayer that this is God's will. . . ."*

The reality is that when we try to discern God's will, we never objectively and tangibly know for certain what God's will is. But that doesn't mean that we shouldn't passionately pursue God's will in prayer. Persistence in prayer slowly reveals glimpses of God's will. These glimpses come through inspirations, conversations, actions, and providences. Just because we don't fully know what God's will is doesn't mean that prayerfully pursuing God's will won't reveal God's will. When we honestly seek God's will, especially together, we discover that God's will finds a way to work. We find that God finds a way to help us realize what God's will is in the end.

As it says in Proverbs: *"Trust in the Lord with all your heart, and do not rely on your own insight. In all your ways acknowledge* [God], *and* [God] *will make straight your paths"* (3:5–6).

Proverb 26.

In the event of a church or leadership crisis, get your own oxygen first before assisting others.

CHURCHES GO THROUGH CRISES all the time. Pastors go through crises all the time. People go through crises all the time. As much as we like to think that churches should be places of calm, peace, and joy, they often aren't. In fact, churches are often places for crises. Why?

They are because churches have a calling to help people in crisis. When someone dies, the pastor(s) and church members are there to help families through their crisis. When natural disasters hit, it's often churches and their denominations that are the first to respond and the last to leave. When people's lives start to fall apart, often they turn to the church for help. When people have no homes, no food, no resources, churches are often the first places people look to for help because churches generally will help.

Still, churches are flawed human institutions. So they end up with all sorts of internal crises that rise up out of the same kinds of conflict that afflict every human endeavor. People in churches (including some pastors) may pursue power, hoping to become big fish in small ponds. Their pursuit can create crises. Church people (pastors included) are often dysfunctional simply because, as good as they yearn to be, they come from dysfunctional backgrounds. Their tendency to either be in perpetual conflict, or to avoid conflict in a way that creates more conflict (see Proverb 9), can spread conflict. Remember, churches attract broken people, so it shouldn't surprise anyone that broken people in churches can act, well, broken.

How should pastors and church leaders act in a crisis? Flight attendants have the answer. Before takeoff, flight attendants say, "In the event of a decompression, an oxygen mask will automatically appear in front of you. To start the flow of oxygen, pull the mask toward you. Place it firmly over your nose and mouth, secure the elastic band behind your head, and breathe normally. Although the bag does not inflate, oxygen is flowing to the mask. If you are travelling with a child or someone who requires assistance, secure your mask first, and then assist the other person." In other words, if this plane is in crisis, get your own oxygen first before helping others.

The same advice is good in churches. We can't help other people unless we first attend to ourselves. We have to do the best we can to put ourselves in a good place before responding to others. So, if we are in a meeting where people are becoming angry, we need to find a way to calm ourselves first before we respond. Otherwise we will respond in anger or fear, which creates more anger and fear. If we find ourselves in a dysfunctional situation, we need to step back as best we can, center ourselves in God's presence, and return with a sense of calm rather than tension. If our church is in crisis, it may be helpful to take time off for a few hours or days to center, seek wise counsel, and get a sense of how God is calling us to respond. Then we move back into the crisis. In general we can't minister to others unless we also minister to ourselves.

Getting our own oxygen first means becoming open to God's Spirit so that we can acquire a sense of calm and wisdom, and only then move back to trying to help others. This is the example of Pentecost. The early Christians were in crisis, but they waited for the Holy Spirit before acting. They also spent an inordinate amount of time in prayer so that they could be prepared to prayerfully help others.

Too often pastors get in a crisis situation, and add to the crisis via their own responses to fear: flight, fight, or freeze. By centering and connecting with God—by getting our own oxygen first—we can instead choose a course based on faith, not fear.

Proverb 27.

*When leading a church, learn the great secret that
"everything matters; nothing matters."*

Y EARS AGO I CAME ACROSS THIS PARADOX: *everything
matters; nothing maters.* I found it in the pages of the
book, *A Testament of Devotion,*[1] by the great Quaker
mystic, Thomas Kelly. It changed my whole perspective on
ministry and life. In many ways this small phrase holds the
secret to becoming an effective leader not only of a church,
but of almost any endeavor.

We live in a narcissistic culture. There's a tremendous
amount of self-importance to everything we see, hear, and do—
from political opinions to reality television to Internet blogs to
the sense people have of their place in the world. There's also
a tremendous amount of spiritual, theological, and religious
narcissism. Whether it is the fundamentalist Christian who is
convinced that only she or he knows the true path to salvation,
or the fundamentalist atheist who believes that only he or she
understands the true nature of life, narcissists abound.

Narcissism kills leadership, despite the fact that many
narcissists aspire to be leaders. It kills leadership because
narcissistic leaders think everything they do has cosmic significance, while they treat those around them as though they
are cosmically insignificant. At the same time, feeling unduly
insignificant also kills leadership. Many people struggle as
leaders because they worry that no matter what they do, it
doesn't matter. They can't change the world, so why bother.
They want to matter, but they fear that neither they nor their

---

1. Thomas R. Kelly, *A Testament of Devotion* (San Francisco: HarperSan-
Francisco, 1992): 40.

efforts matter. So, their crisis of confidence kills their leadership. Enter our paradox: *everything matters; nothing matters.*

This paradox holds the key to truly meaningful ministry. Everything we do really does matter. When we embark on any endeavor to serve God, we need to realize that there is some cosmic significance in what we are doing because we are serving God; and God is cosmically significant to the nth degree. Unfortunately, once we think that what we are doing has universal significance, that's the moment our ministry has become diminished. If we think that the fate of the world depends upon our Bible study, small group, mission work to Africa, sermon, worship service, choir piece, strawberry festival, the color of carpet we choose for our church hall, or the color of paint in our sanctuary . . . it doesn't.

The universe is almost completely unaware of what we are doing. So we need to realize that even though we think that everything we do matters, nothing we do really matters. We need to approach everything we do with humility, recognizing that in a world of seven billion people, nothing we do really matters that much.

Yet the moment we begin to believe that nothing we do matters, we have to realize that to God everything we do does matter. God deeply cares about what we do. God actually cares about the color of carpet in our church hall, the paint in our sanctuary, the strawberry festival, our sermon, and our Bible study, if their point is to help people encounter and serve God. They have eternal significance and matter a great deal. So even if we think that what we do doesn't really matter, we need to realize that it does.

Good leadership approaches ministry and mission as though it has cosmic significance, which means doing what we do to the best of our abilities. But it always approaches ministry and mission with a sense of mercy and modesty that treats those we are serving, and those who serve with us, with compassion. We live out what Paul teaches: "*Do nothing from selfish ambition or conceit, but in humility regard others as better than yourselves. Let each of you look not to your own interests, but to the interests of others"* (Philippians 2:3–4).

Ultimately, the paradox of *everything matters; nothing matters* means doing what we do with maximum effort, but minimum ego. The balance of everything and nothing mattering at the same time allows us to always do our best work, while having a sense of humility about it. We don't worry whether or not we are changing the world. We are content with whatever impact we have. We can act grandly without becoming grandiose, serve humbly without feeling humiliated, do great things without needing to be great, and do small things without feeling small.

Leading others out of *everything matters; nothing matters* allows us to lead in a way that takes seriously what we are doing, while living joyfully as we do.

Proverb 28.

*Churches constantly battle entropy, which leads
to apathy, which leads to atrophy. Churches
can only overcome entropy with spiritual energy.
If they restore the Spirit, they can multiply; if not,
they will simply gentrify.*

ENTROPY ISN'T A FAMILIAR TERM for most pastors and
church leaders, but we all know what it is anyway.
Entropy causes our aging bodies to wrinkle and sag. It
causes fires to die out, nights to get colder, ice to melt, athletes to
retire, cars to rust, trees to rot, and every living creature to die.

What is entropy? It's a term from physics referring to
the second law of thermodynamics. Simply put, it says
that all energy systems—galaxies, stars, planets, creatures,
everything—will eventually run down. Ultimately, all existing
things slowly convert to a lower energy state. Your body goes
south over time because your body can't maintain the same
energy levels it did when you were a kid, teen, or young adult.
We gain weight over time because of this energy drain. We eat
more sweet and salty carbohydrates because they give us an
energy rush, even though the weight gain they cause actually
decreases energy, leaving us to feel tired all the time.

Churches are afflicted by entropy. Typically churches
begin with high energy—an energy and excitement that can
last years as the church grows. Eventually, that energy lags.
The members get older. The pastor(s) get older. The surrounding community gets older. The focus becomes more on maintaining rather than growing. Creativity slowly erodes, and
doing what we always have done becomes our goal.

As the church lags, the members become more apathetic.
The pastor(s) become more apathetic. They complain about

the apathy, but that only leads to more apathy. And the frustrated sermons about everyone's apathy spark little sympathy as the church begins to atrophy. Members die. Few new members join. Mission declines. Ministry declines. Giving declines. Ultimately, the church in atrophy begins to gentrify as it just gets older. The saddest part is when the church has to close because its young members are all in their 60s. The pastors and church leaders sense the decline, but they feel helpless to stem the energy loss. They try new programs, read books, try new ventures, but the church's decline continues. Why?

The decline continues because the leaders don't tap into the only thing that can really reverse entropy, which is spiritual energy. The church began as a calling by the Holy Spirit to reach out to the community. But as the church experienced the decline of entropy-apathy-atrophy-gentrify, they forgot about the Spirit. They forgot that the early church's wonderful energy came from the coming of the Spirit on Pentecost. No new program will work if it isn't preceded by prayer and openness to the Spirit, or if it does it's only temporary.

So what's the answer? Becoming more open to the Spirit by increasing prayer, by leaders seeking the Spirit's guidance, and by trusting in the Spirit to bring people with greater energy to the church. The only way to grow again is to grow in the Spirit, and to let the Spirit's energy overcome the power of entropy.

On a practical level it means simple things: pastors who pray alone and with others for the Spirit to inspire, and who do so regularly. It means leaders who pray regularly and are open to the Spirit's guidance. We live in a time in which many pastors and church leaders want to be grounded in the example of the early church, but they leave out the deep devotion to prayer and Spirit found all through the Book of Acts.

If we become deeply open to the Spirit, our churches can multiply again, but if we don't, they will gentrify and eventually mummify as they become relics of the past. Or worse, they zombify as they become the church of the walking dead.

Proverb 29.

*Churches become healthy when they know
"why" they do "what" they do. When what we
do is based on a clear "why," we act with purpose.
When we don't know why we do what we do,
we lose our focus.*

W HY DO SOME CHURCHES FLOURISH and others struggle? Those that flourish generally know *why* they do what they do. Those that struggle typically only know *what* they do.

Simon Sinek, in his viral TED video and book, *Start with Why*,[1] describes how some organizations become great and others struggle. His insights about businesses, entrepreneurial ventures, and organizations apply prophetically to churches. Too many of our churches only understand *what* they are doing. They have no real clue as to *why* they are doing it.

Why do we continue to host the strawberry festival year after year, when few people come anymore? Why do we insist on playing mostly the same hymns today that were sung in the 1950s? Why do we insist on saying "We've always done it this way," when clearly that way is no longer working because people are no longer coming?

Most mainline churches are expert in knowing *what* to do, but they're generally lost as to *why* they do what they do. And understanding *why* is the key to health, growth, and renewal. *Why* is vision. It is the ability to understand where we want to go (or more specifically, where we are *called* to go), and what our purpose is in doing it. When we understand clearly why

---

1. Simon Sinek, *Start with Why: How Great Leaders Inspire Everyone to Take Action* (New York: Penguin Group, 2009).

we are doing what we are doing, and when this *why* is based on a compelling purpose, then it leads to creative, dynamic, and inspiring ministry and mission.

Unfortunately, many pastors and church leaders with vision are great at understanding why, but stink at actually figuring out what needs to be done to accomplish their "why." This is the struggle for many seminary theologians who are good at saying what the church's purpose is (in other words, the *why* underlying a church's ministry and mission), but can't tell people how to pragmatically accomplish it. This problem extends to many pastors who have strong, deeply held convictions and theologies about a church's purpose, but never manage to articulate how to accomplish what they want the church to do. They are good at offering "shoulds" and "oughts," but terrible at offering pragmatic "hows" that accomplish what we "should" and "ought" to do.

Meanwhile, a bigger problem is that most churches and pastors are good at articulating *what* we should do as a church, but never really understand or articulate *why* we should do it. Why should we worship this way over that way? Is it simply because that's our tradition? Why is our board structured the way it is, and is this the best way to create a leadership team? Why do we engage in the ministries and missions that we do? If we are good at articulating *what* to do, but then don't have a compelling, inspirational *why* at the core of what we do, then what we do will cease to inspire our members, and the ministries and missions will founder.

Ultimately, leading a healthy church requires being able to articulate both *why* and *what*. We need to be clear about why we should engage in a ministry, but also articulate and plan out specific and concrete steps to achieve it.

A simple way of thinking about this is that apostles always understood why they were spreading the gospel. They knew that they were called by God to reach out in Christ's love. That was their purpose, their calling, and their why. At the same time, they knew concretely what to do and how to do it: preach, teach, heal, feed, create communities, love each other, and do so in ways that were relevant to each kind of person.

Do we know *why* we do what we do, and do we know concretely *what* to do based on that *why*?

Proverb 30.

*When doing pastoral care we need to ask,
"Am I here simply to listen, or to help solve a
problem?" If we merely listen when a problem needs
to be solved, we increase helplessness. If we try to
solve a problem when someone just wants to be
heard, we increase frustration.*

I N MOST PASTORS' PASTORAL CARE TRAINING, they are taught to listen. It's quite common to be taught that our primary task is to be a caring presence, to incarnate the compassion of Christ, and to be the face of love. Every single one of those tasks is important and necessary, especially in a world where very few people really listen to each other, and very few people ever feel really heard. Pastors are called to care, especially in the face of helplessness.

Unfortunately, pastors can sometimes be so intent on listening that they don't know when it is time to help solve a problem. We can focus so much on listening that we forget the importance of doing.

At the same time, there are some pastors who love to give advice, who love to intervene in people's lives, and who love to help people tangibly—but they never really listen. They focus so much on intervening that they forget the gift of listening.

There's a tension between listening and intervening. And the line between the two is not always clear. It's pretty clear when listening to someone in advanced age struggling with an aging body. There's not much we can do about the fact that she or he is no longer young. Listening becomes a gift because it shows that someone understands and loves the person. On the other hand, if someone comes to us because she or he has no food, just listening and saying "I understand how hard it is to be hungry" isn't much of a response. The person needs food, not an ear.

Confusion arises as we move into the gray areas. What about a person who is having conflict with a family member that is tearing the family apart? What about someone who has breaking and rotting teeth, but can't afford the $7,000 it would take to fix her teeth? What about the person suffering from depression who has no health insurance to pay for counseling and medication? What about the person who has lost his job, can't find a new one, and seems to lack interviewing skills? What about the person who hates his job and is becoming increasingly depressed as a result?

So many of our pastoral situations walk the line between listening and intervening. What makes it worse is that some people come to us acting as though they want advice, but they really just want to be heard. We can tell because they often play a game of "yeah, but"—responding to any advice with, "Yeah, I tried doing that, but it didn't work" or "Yeah, that's a good idea, but I doubt my mother would ever consider it." Trying to intervene with these people irritates them and frustrates us.

Other times people act as though they simply want to be heard, but they really want our help. These are people who will tell us about their problems in drips and dribbles, but then downplay their problems. They want tangible help, but they are reluctant to ask, so they act as though they are just telling their story. If we merely listen to them, we increase their sense of helplessness and our own sense of irrelevance.

It takes wisdom to tell when it's time to listen and when it's time to intervene, but it also takes resources. Too often we don't create the right resources to help people in times of struggle. We can marshal many efforts toward mission in far-flung places, or even in the community, but the ability to help someone in need requires the ability to pastorally care enough to do something when something needs to be done.

Jesus was a great example of that. He would often listen to people, or silently care, such as when the woman anointed him with oil and washed his feet with her tears and hair (Luke 7:38). But just as often Jesus marshaled his resources: he healed, he fed, he changed water into wine, he offered wisdom and guidance, he embraced, he wept, and so much more.

The key to caring for people pastorally is in developing the prayerful wisdom to know the right way to respond when someone comes to us in turmoil.

Proverb 31.

*If the church isn't growing, it's dying, because the
nature of life is to grow. And once it starts dying,
the only answer is to prune and nourish: prune what
is dying, and nourish what may grow.*

HOW DO YOU GET A PLANT TO GROW to a perfect size,
and then get it to stop? How do you make sure
that it never outgrows its pot, never has too many
blooms, or never does anything it hasn't done before? How do
you get a plant to stay the way it is—the way you like it best?

It's incredibly difficult to keep plants, or any living things,
to stay the way they are. The nature of living things is to grow.
Even if we're talking about a Japanese bonsai tree, it wants to
grow. You can tend a bonsai and try to keep it from growing,
but the amount of energy and attention needed is intensive.
Why? Because the tree desperately wants to grow. To keep it
from growing we have to do three times the work of pruning,
misting, managing the soil, and tinkering with the roots.

Like any tree, churches are living organisms, not bonsai.
They are meant to grow. The problem is that so many members of our modern churches really want their churches to
stay the same. While most pastors and church leaders would
like their churches to grow, there's often a lot of resistance to
it. I found this out by pastoring a growing church.

As our church grew, I began to hear complaints from lon-
ger-term members: "I don't know anyone in church anymore.
I miss the days when we'd come into the sanctuary and know
everyone." Of course, the reason everyone knew everyone
else was that it had been shrinking for twenty-five years. We
even had some members leave because they didn't like the fact
that the church was growing. Ironically, most went to other

churches, where they really knew nobody. They would rather go to a church where nobody knew their names, or go nowhere, than share their church and learn new members' names.

Churches really are meant to grow, but we often don't do the things that let them grow. We let fear of offending people, fear of changing hymns, fear of members leaving, and fear of being criticized prevent our churches from growing. All of this fear causes us to treat our churches like bonsai, as we exert tremendous energy in keeping everything the same.

What allows churches to grow naturally are people who are seeking spiritual growth. A fair number of people outside of churches want to grow spiritually, but they don't find avenues for spiritual growth within our churches. The reason is that too many of our churches haven't been seeking to offer spiritual growth. They've been seeking stability, which leads to stagnation over time.

How do we help churches grow? The same way we help plants grow. If a plant starts to bud a flower, we don't put a cap on it, forcing the plant to wait until we can have a committee meeting and then a board meeting to determine if the bud should flower. We let it grow. In churches, that means that when someone has an idea for ministry or mission, especially if it feels like a calling, we don't send it to a committee, then send it to the board, only to send it back three months later with permission. Instead, we immediately try to help the idea grow. We say yes to the idea (within reason—as long as it is in harmony with the church's vision), and then let our committees and boards figure out how to support the ministry and mission.

Some of our most successful ministries have been the result of someone in our congregation sensing a call to do something and our finding resources to nurture that ministry. If someone wants to start a small group, we help them find resources rather than forcing them to seek permission from the board. If someone wants to start an unemployment support group, we find a room for them to meet and resources to help them run workshops and networking programs. If someone wants to join the mission of another church to go to Africa, we send out pleas to the congregation to raise money supporting the trip. If people feel a calling to transform worship, we work with them to transform worship in a way that reaches out to people like them. In other words, when a flower begins to bud, we nurture its growth.

In the same way, if a plant has too many dead leaves and stems, we prune them to allow more energy to go toward growth instead of death. If the Strawberry Festival, the Trash and Treasures Sale, the graduate recognition dinner, the music we use in worship, or the way we light the Advent wreath is no longer working, prune them so that new growth can occur. It's painful to prune, but it allows for growth.

Taking a metaphor from Jesus's parables, it's like vines growing to make wine. Vinegrowers intentionally prune back the grape vines to allow more energy to be devoted to growing the fruit. Great grapes require both nurturing and pruning. Plants won't grow to be healthy if we also won't prune what's struggling or dying.

The point is that churches naturally grow; at one point all of our churches grew. The question is whether we are allowing that growth to occur.

Proverb 32.

*We should seek simplicity and naturality in all that
we do in a church. There is a natural way of being
simple, and a simple way of being natural. And when
churches become more naturally simple, they grow.*

T OO OFTEN CHURCHES, THEIR MINISTRIES, and their
mission get lost in complexity. Complexity can kill
faith, and complexity can kill churches . . . or at
least diminish them.

The reality is that all of life is complex. Look at a leaf and
its structure. It is terribly complex, but at the same time its
nature is simple. Its beauty lies in its apparent simplicity that
paradoxically conceals its complexity. If a leaf were incredibly
pixelated, with nobs and nibs creating a mess, it would both
become inefficient and inelegant. We'd rarely stop to contemplate it.

All of nature has a simplicity to it that inspires awe. It's
what draws us to contemplate it. But what amazes us is its
naturality. No matter how complex it gets, it feels naturally
simple. We can grasp it, even if we don't understand it.

Churches often lose the natural in complexity. Our boards
follow complex procedures that don't feel natural. What feels
natural about a discussion that keeps breaking down into the
addition of one amendment after another? What feels natural
about making a motion, or seconding a motion? What feels
natural about lofty prayers straight out of the nineteenth century, sacraments choreographed from a book, ministry and
mission ideas that have to go through layers and layers of
committees before possibly seeing the light of day, and sermons that explore so many ideas that listeners can't figure out
what the basic message is?

People thrive most when life becomes natural and simple. Churches flourish when they feel natural and simple. Sermons bear fruit when they feel natural and simple. All of this does not mean that people, churches, and preaching thrive when they are simplistic. Being simplistic means being reductionistic. It attempts to get rid of complexity by denying it and pretending it isn't there. Simplicity captures the complex and deepens it by making it easily grasped and embraced.

For example, atheists treat faith in a simplistic way when they claim that religion is merely a crutch for people who are afraid of reality. They reduce religion to formulas based on an unnatural rationality, or a fear of dying. Jesus captures the essence of faith simply and naturally when he says that we should love the Lord our God with all of our mind, heart, soul, and strength, and others as ourselves. This command captures the heart of Christian religion. Do this, and the rest will follow.

To be simple and natural in our approach to ministry means to look for ways to cut through the complexity of church to make it more about simply serving God as part of a living church body, rather than merely serving the institution. It means cutting through the complexity of theology in sermons by using simple stories and metaphors to help people capture the heart of the idea. It means finding ways to allow relationships to flow and grow. It is also the key to good teaching: make the complex feel simple and natural so that people can grasp ideas with their hearts, and not just their minds.

To make things feel simpler and more natural is a key to nurturing growth in a church.

Proverb 33.

All churches create self-fulfilling prophecies about themselves. The question is what kind they will create: a prophecy of struggle, turmoil, and decline, or one of love, passion, and growth?

BACK WHEN I WAS A KID, we had an exchange student from India stay at our house who said he could read palms. As a gullible ten year old, I was anxious to find out my future. So he read my palm and told me that I would have one wife and one child. I asked him how he knew, and he showed me the lines on the side of my left hand that supposedly predicted such things.

So, when I grew to dating age, I was determined to find that one woman who would have only that one child with me. I don't want to make it sound as though this was my primary dating criteria, but it always lurked in the background. I would find a way to secretly, or at least not obviously, check the hand lines of a girlfriend at some point to see if she had similar lines to mine, demonstrating that she was *the one*. If she didn't have the proper lines, it put a definite crimp in our relationship, although I never quite told her that. It became part of my secret reasoning for why the relationship didn't last: "How could it have, her palm said she would have two marriages and three children?"

In essence, the exchange student had made a hand-fulfilling prophecy about me that I then proceeded to make sure came true. I was crafting my life to fit his prophecy.

I was an idiot, I know! I never broke up over my reading of anyone's palm, but it didn't help. Once I read a girlfriend's palm, it made it easier to be disappointed if things didn't work out. If we had an argument, I would silently say to myself, "Of course, it's because she's not *the one*."

What I was doing was not only stupid, but it was mildly self-destructive. I was letting a palm reading determine the direction of my life. It didn't matter if the prediction was true or false; I was subtly crafting my life to fit it. I was only going to have one wife and one child (I've had only one wife, but I have two children), which then influenced the success of my relationships.

A self-fulfilling prophecy is a strongly held belief or prediction that we make sure comes true—even if a better outcome is possible. We see the problems of self-fulfilling prophecies a lot in counseling. We will get a client who believes that she is a failure, and as a result ends up with a failing life. Her life doesn't fail because failing is inevitable. She fails because her belief in her own failure sabotages the possibility of success. We become what we believe we will become. We can also see this in work situations where a person believes he can't do the job, and so he self-sabotages, even if he actually has the skills to do the job.

Churches and their leaders generally have self-fulfilling prophecies about their churches and themselves. Some churches believe that they will always struggle, attract poorly skilled pastors, and never be attractive to outsiders. Some pastors believe that their churches will always struggle, be poorly skilled, and never be attractive to outsiders. They think it's inevitable. As a result, they end up combining to create low-energy, struggling churches to fulfill their prophecies.

Churches that do well believe that they can do well. They see their future as unlimited. Their pastors believe that their churches are the greatest churches on earth, and as a result the churches become great churches in terms of relationships, leadership, ministry, and mission. They become dynamic churches where people are caring and active.

The point is that no church is destined for failure or success, but what we predict about our churches and ourselves often determines success or failure. I believe that God actually wants all of our churches to do well, but if we believe they won't, God won't force the churches to do well. In essence, what we believe is what we become.

Proverb 34.

When we preach, if we are not focused on
transforming people, we merely inform people.
And when we merely inform people, the best we
can be is merely interesting. But when we focus on
forming people, we can transform them.

M OST PASTORS LOVE TO PREACH. Why? Is it the opportunity to get people who would normally ignore us
to listen to us? Do we love the opportunity to think
deeper than normal? Do we love having the opportunity to
explore deep theological ideas? Why do we love to preach?

Many pastors I've spoken with tell me that they love
thinking theologically and that they love the opportunity to
share theological thoughts with others. In essence, they had
been moved by the theological exploration of pastors and
professors in the past, and they hope to help others experience
something similar.

Unfortunately, the focus on teaching theology is also what
has turned many people off to religion. They don't want theological information. They want personal transformation. Many
who come to church struggle with their lives. They don't feel
as though their lives are in order. They feel as though God is
absent, or at least on holiday, while they struggle with issues
that never seem to get resolved. They've tried praying, but they
feel inadequate. They have questions—deep questions—but
these generally aren't questions about the nature of God, the
Trinity, the atonement, creation, the nature of sin, the delay of
the parousia (Christ's return), or the number of other topics
that many of us love to explore theologically.

Their questions are more practical, but also more transformational in nature. They want to know where God is and

how to live lives that are wiser, better, happier, and filled with a greater sense of God's presence. They also want to know how to make their lives more fulfilling and joyful. They don't necessarily articulate their questions in this way, but the flood of people fleeing our theologically oriented churches suggests that we are on the wrong track in terms of what questions we address. We are addressing questions they aren't asking. If we spend time reviewing writings by non-Christian spiritual writers, it's clear that those who have left the church are seeking formation (the shaping of their lives in a healthy way) rather than just theological information about Jesus, the Bible, and what we believe.

In short, people seeking answers want to be transformed. They want to find a way out of the lives they are living, which feel inadequate, into lives that seem more fulfilling. So the question is, when we preach, are we giving people theological information that fulfills a dogmatic checklist of things to say, or are we leading them into spiritual transformation based on an encounter with God?

Before you misinterpret what I'm saying as an attack on theological thinking, please understand that I do consider a strong theological foundation to be important. If we don't have that foundation, we crumble. But we are trying to help people build houses with God, and continually focusing on the foundation doesn't put a roof up, walls around, windows in, or flooring down. People want to be transformed from the ramshackle lives they live into ones filled with love, hope, and a sense of God's presence. Theology provides a foundation, but they want more.

How does this translate into preaching? I think that many Protestant pastors love to explore existential problems without offering a pathway beyond the problems. They love to describe what's wrong with our lives without offering pragmatic, spiritually rich ways to overcome or resolve the problems. They love to explore our individual or collective sins,

or the sins of everyone "out there" (non-churchgoers, politi-
cians, the government, drug addicts, extremists, progressives,
conservatives, racists, corporations, those who love violence,
and a whole collection of others), but they forget to point people toward how to find love and God's grace in the minute
moments of life.

Transformational preaching helps people to quit thinking
about God by helping them to connect *with* God. It asks the
questions, "How will people tangibly be different after listening to my sermon? Will they be better equipped to deal with
the struggles of life? Will they find God in the struggles? Will
they be better able to love others and be loved? Will they be
transforming presences themselves?"

Ultimately, transformational preaching understands a
little-appreciated fact about the gospels. While they have
plenty of theology, history, and teachings, their main focus
is on spiritual transformation. Jesus had a fairly simple
message: real change in life and the world comes by being
radically available to God. This focus cuts through conservative and progressive mindsets. It's the idea that when we
open up to God, God changes the way we think, behave,
and live. We become more compassionate and hopeful, and
less of what we were without God. Conservatives become
more progressive. Progressives become more conservative.
Morality-minded Christians become more social justice oriented, and social justice Christians become more morality
minded. Why? Because they've let God transform them into
what God is calling them to be. It is achieving something the
Eastern Orthodox tradition emphasizes, which is that even
though we are created in God's image, we are also called to
constantly grow into Christ's likeness.

In essence, transformational preaching doesn't teach us
how to change ourselves. It teaches us how to become available to God so that God can transform us into what God is
calling us to be.

Proverb 35.

Ministry is about loving others, but love needs boundaries. When we have no boundaries, we can easily be manipulated because manipulators love to manipulate those who love.

ONE OF THE MOST DIFFICULT and persistent problems for pastors and churches is figuring out what to do about strangers who ask for money. Some churches have to deal with this issue a lot, others only periodically. But whether it's a lot or a little, how we respond creates a conundrum. The reality is that some (certainly not all) of the people who seek our help are both really needy and really good cons. They genuinely need help, yet they are manipulators who have learned that people's genuine compassion and care can be twisted to their advantage.

As a pastor, I've been conned many times. And I've been conned because the cons, despite their manipulation, are in need. They've fallen on bad times. They've had genuinely bad situations. One man I helped for several years had been falsely convicted of rape and spent five years in prison. By the time he was released, he had little money and few resources. Despite his innocence, he had a hard time finding a job. So his job became using his false imprisonment and subsequent struggles as a lure to get people to help him. We discovered, over time, that we were one of a number of churches that were helping him, and his full-time job had become keeping us all unaware and in his constellation.

Another person had worked as a roofer and had injured his back falling off a roof. His injuries became chronic. He had a hard time finding work. His wife left him with two children because she didn't want to support them. So he discovered that he could use his plight to convince churches to help him out so that he could house and feed his family. Over time, though, he quit looking for a job because using his plight to obtain tax-free support became his job. Again, he kept a number of churches in his circle of help, but he made sure we didn't know that all of us were helping him. He went from a man in need to a man of manipulation.

In both of these cases, we eventually had to stop helping them because we were being asked for more and more. When we tried to stop, the second man changed his tactic a bit. He made sure he showed up to our church unannounced with his oxygen tank and ten-year-old daughter in tow to pluck at our compassion. That worked for a bit. Nothing evokes compassion like a doe-eyed daughter and oxygen.

We had another person who came to me consistently for counseling and spiritual guidance. He had legitimate issues and needed guidance. I wasn't alone in my work with him. I insisted that he also seek mental health treatment. Eventually, though, I had to stop working with him because he was requiring more and more attention. I would receive three, four, five phone calls a week asking to talk. That was on top of the fifteen weekly emails and the one-and-a-half-hour sessions we were having every other week. It was painful to tell him that I couldn't help as much anymore, but it was clear that he wanted my attention more than he wanted to change. This was a different kind of manipulation—a desire for attention rather than real help in changing his life.

We are taught as Christians that love is boundless, but if we don't set boundaries, love becomes a trap. That's what's so difficult about loving those in need: they need our love, but may abuse our love. Learning to create boundaries for our love is a really painful lesson.

I have developed a rule: "When in doubt, err in love." Too many pastors and churches err on the side of self-protection and skepticism. We have to remember that even those conning us generally do so because they need help. Manipulation is the skill set they've learned to fill in the gaps where the failures of the social safety net, the lack of employment possibilities, and a lack of hope meet.

At the same time, we can't care more about them than they care about themselves. Love has to have boundaries. If we care about people more than they care about themselves, then we open ourselves to being conned and manipulated. Sometimes pulling back and letting them struggle can be the most loving thing to do. The key is knowing when to err on the side of love without boundaries, and when to pull back and set up boundaries.

Proverb 36.

*Love and trust are the most important qualities
of healthy churches. When congregations feel loved
and trusted by pastors, they can accomplish almost
anything. When they feel unloved and distrusted,
they will struggle, snipe, and stagnate.*

PRIOR TO GOING TO SEMINARY and becoming a pastor, I worked as a therapist with children and teens in a psychiatric hospital. It was an eye-opening experience. There were a number of teens and children who had baffling disorders such as schizophrenia, obsessive-compulsive disorder, and bipolar disorder. The vast majority of the kids, though, seemed to suffer from problems that didn't neatly fit into a diagnostic category.

Some had tried to commit suicide. Others had pretended to try to commit suicide. Some had tried to set their schools on fire. Others had persistent family problems that led to constant arguing and self-abusive behavior. Others just had a multitude of problems that made treatment difficult. And sometimes it seemed that they were brought to us to get them away from their families for a while.

We would put them on a behavior modification program, offer group therapy once a week, family therapy once a week, individual therapy once a day, and medication. Over time, through my work as an individual therapist and behavioral modification specialist, it became very apparent to me that what a significant number of them lacked was something we couldn't really provide. A significant number of them just didn't feel loved by their parents, families, or anyone else. It was hard to objectively tell whether they just didn't *feel* loved or if they actually *weren't* loved, but the outcome was the same. They didn't feel loved, and their behavioral problems were generally an attempt to be noticed, if not loved. When we say that suicidal acts, acting out, and risky behavior are attempts at getting attention, that explanation falls short of what they really are. They really are acts of people who feel unloved and distrusted, who are either crying for help or are pushing people away because they are crying from the pain.

My experiences at the hospital have had a lasting impact on me, not only as a therapist, but as a pastor. I realized many years ago that, like those teens and children, a significant number of our churches feel unloved by their pastors. Pastors may talk a good game about how they value church members, but congregations know when their pastors really don't love them.

Pastors may *like* their churches. They may empathize with their churches, but many pastors don't *love* their churches the way they love their children or other family members. And in a number of churches the pastors have a fair amount of dislike, scorn, or even contempt for their churches. There are a number of reasons for their lack of love.

For some pastors, it may simply be that they have set goals for themselves, and they see their church as one in a series of stepping stones to a bigger church, which they will really love once they get there. For them it's hard to love a stepping stone.

Some pastors move into their new congregations not so much to love as hoping to be loved. When the church (especially if it's had bad experiences with pastors before) doesn't offer the hoped-for love, the pastor then begins to minister out of hurt and disappointment. In essence, the pastor says, "How can I love a church that doesn't love me?" Unfortunately, pastors are called into ministry to love, not to be loved. Besides, if we don't know how to love, how can we be loved?

Others just aren't good at love. They see ministry as a job filled with sermons to preach, people to visit, meetings to attend, and many things to do. When ministry is just another job, the church will be just another social organization.

The point is that "God is love, and those who abide in love abide in God, and God abides in them" (1 John 4:16). Churches are meant to be places of love, but if their leaders and pastors don't love them, how are they going to learn to love others, just as if our parents don't love us, how are we going to learn to love others? As pastors and leaders, loving and trusting our churches helps them grow in awareness of God, for "love is from God; everyone who loves is born of God and knows God" (1 John 4:7).

If we want our churches to be filled with dysfunction— with sniping, backbiting, criticism, skepticism, resistance, defensiveness, power grabs, and a functionalism that treats the church like any other nonprofit organization or business— then show them little or no love. But if we want our churches to thrive, all it takes is deciding that we will love our churches, and the people of our churches, no matter what they do. Do this, and we will discover our churches becoming places of striving, thriving, giving, and living.

Proverb 37.

The church needs to tell people why *they believe more than* what *they believe. Sharing* why *tells our story and invites people to experience God. Sharing* what *we believe merely invites them to decide whether or not they agree with our dogma.*

M OST CHURCHES, FOLLOWING TYPICAL BUSINESS and organizational models, spend a lot of time crafting belief statements, faithfully saying *what* their churches believe. They devote whole pages on their websites so that interested church shoppers can know what beliefs lie at the core of their churches. And why not? Aren't we part of traditions that carved out strong beliefs in the beginning? Actually, most of us belong to traditions that fought the church to allow experiences—experiences of the living Word when reading Scripture, experiences of the Holy Spirit in prayer, and experiences of Christ personally after their surrender to Christ. They gained followers because of the experiences they offered seekers.

Our theological beliefs are an important part of describing who we are. This is especially important if we are part of a creedal tradition, where creeds and confessions articulate our beliefs; an evangelical tradition that is proud of its orthodoxy; or a progressive tradition that strives to lift up the oppressed and marginalized. We want to tell people what our faith rests upon. We want to tell potential visitors who they will be worshiping with when they visit.

So, we tell them what our denomination believes. We tell them what our church believes. And in the process, we often give them a ton of information that doesn't really interest them. No matter how well we articulate our beliefs, most people don't care that much about *what* we believe. They want to know *why* we believe.

So many people have left the church because of the over-arching emphasis on "right" belief. They have been part of churches with strongly held beliefs, but have found them also to be stagnant, uncaring, and more concerned with being right than with being caring and compassionate. And people outside of our churches who really haven't grown up in our churches often see our beliefs as being overly dogmatic at best, or hypo-critical and judgmental at worst.

Look back at the early church. It didn't spread because of the logical articulations of Christian belief. In fact, many of the Romans made fun of the Christian faith because its beliefs seemed so illogical. But the faith grew exponentially anyway. Why? Because the early Christians didn't emphasize *what* they believed. They emphasized *why* they believed. Cer-tainly over time they crafted creeds and faith statements, but the *why* always preceded the *what*.

The early Christians talked of their experiences. The apos-tles shared their experiences of Christ first—his miracles, his love, his acceptance, his forgiveness—and then went on to share his teachings. Their followers, who gave their lives to Christ and opened themselves up to the Holy Spirit, spoke about their experiences of Christ and the Spirit. They talked of their experiences of being healed, forgiven, loved, and led. They spoke of how their lives were made better. They spoke of how they were feeling joy despite the pain of life. The early Chris-tians shared their experiences. They said *why* they believed in Christ and were joining the new Christian communities.

When people look for a new church, they want to know why we have been going to our particular church. They want to sense that people in our churches experience God. They want to know what those experiences are. They want to trust that if they visit our churches, they will experience God's pres-ence, light, and love, too.

The only people who care about *what* we believe are those who are either looking for whom to scratch off their list because they're not good enough for them, or who are looking for people who look, think, and act exactly like them.

So when we articulate the faith of our church, tell people *why* the people of our church believe. And if we can't come up with an answer, then perhaps we need to work on creating a church where people can more vibrantly experience God.

Proverb 38.

Don't confuse inspiration and stimulation.
Inspiration comes from connecting people with
God. Stimulation is all about getting people
excited. Settling for stimulation ends up relying
on manipulation. Striving for inspiration ends up
leading people to transformation.

WE LIVE IN STIMULATING TIMES. Everyday life is filled with tremendous stimulation, and when it isn't we seek it. Creating a list of stimulants is easy: smartphones, Internet, Spotify, Pandora, Twitter, Snapchat, iTunes, Netflix, cable TV, radio, iPads, video games, apps and more apps, snack foods, sugar, coffee, alcohol, and unfortunately drugs. That's just the tip of the iceberg. Sure, we all crave down time, but even when we find it, we generally fill it with something stimulating. We can only take so much peace and quiet.

The craving for stimulation has infiltrated the church. Increasingly, churches that draw the most people are those that excel at offering unending stimulation. When we enter their buildings, greeters trained to be friendly and helpful guide us past the coffee shop, soft play area, and gift shop into a full sanctuary of happy worshippers. The service begins with twenty minutes of contemporary Christian music, as worshippers sing, palms raised to the heavens. A rock band plays on a stage, lighted by colored LED spots, backed by flowing slide presentations, all with the sophistication you would expect at an arena concert. The talks/sermons are professionally done, offering self-help guidance for those struggling to make their way through life. Everything about the service is stimulating, exciting, and a feast for the senses.

It's easy for people to become attracted to this kind of worship when compared to our traditional churches, where visitors often enter a church where few people greet them, and they find their way into the sparsely filled sanctuary. The music is soft, as the lone organist plays an 1800s classic. People chat with one another in soft tones. The service begins with a welcome and announcements, but there's not much energy. And while there is some music, the service is mostly spoken or read. Not much in the service is energetic or stimulating. No wonder people are flocking to the contemporary churches. They offer stimulation while we offer stagnation.

The problem is that most of the people going to either of these churches, whether traditional or contemporary, aren't really there for the stimulation. They seek inspiration. They want to experience God in some way. They want their lives to be transformed. They want to feel God's love, grace, and presence. But in the absence of inspiration, people will choose stimulation because they can confuse stimulation with inspiration. Unfortunately this also leaves them open to manipulation because emotional stimulation often serves as an entry into people's lives. Cult leaders, advertisers, con artists, and false prophets have known this for centuries.

What people really seek is an authentic experience of God, which means that we have to ask a foundational question: is what we are offering in worship leading people to be inspired, stimulated, or stagnated? Neither traditional nor contemporary worship is automatically inspiring. Neither is better at offering authentic inspirational experiences. Some people find genuine inspiration from traditional worship, but generally only when the worship itself is intended to lead to an experience of God's Spirit. If the service is just an expression of what we've always done, then it stifles inspiration. Others find genuine inspiration from contemporary worship, but only when the service itself is genuinely intended to inspire people to form a deep connection with Christ.

The secret is the question we ask at the core of our worship: "What's our intention?" Is it to maintain convention? Is it to offer some sort of motivation? Or is it to offer a genuine avenue to inspiration?

Proverb 39.

*What we strive for is what we get. If we strive for
numbers, we get a church of people who like to
follow a crowd. If we strive merely to survive, we get
a church of people who only seek self-preservation.
But if we strive for God, we get a church full
of people who yearn for God.*

WE'VE BECOME A BIT MESSED UP in the goals we've
been setting for our modern churches. What I mean
is that we no longer really know what it is that we
want our churches to be. We've followed so many different
models of ministry over the past fifty years that we're not sure
what we should strive for. What should our models be?

We've tried the counseling model where each pastor is
to lead the church like a group therapist, helping members
become self-actualized and empowering them to become the
best of what they can be. We've tried the political model,
where we act like mini-congresses, debating issues and always
going with the majority rule. We've tried the business model
where we try to become efficient small businesses, cultivating
balanced budgets and offering reasonable products at reasonable prices (in other words, offering nice sermons and services
without asking for too much membership commitment). In
recent years, the marketing model has become a significant
model, as we look for how to develop our brand, advertise,
and entice people to visit.

Each model has its own measuring stick. The group therapy model's success is determined by how many members
are visited and how many groups are formed. The political
model's success is determined by battles won and the sizes
of majorities. The business model's success is determined by

balanced or surplus budgets. The marketing model's success is determined by worship attendance and membership numbers.

In recent years the marketing model has dominated, so contemporary church success stories celebrate how quickly and large the church grew: "We started with five members three years ago, and now we have three thousand!!!!!" The newest model is the missional model, where success may be measured by the number of mission projects and by who outside the church is being served.

What we strive for is eventually what we get. If we strive to be therapeutic, we will create a therapeutic church where what matters is people feeling good about themselves. If we strive to be a political entity, we will accomplish good things, but we will also get the same kind of division that exists in every political body. If we strive to be a business, we will get efficiency and fiscal responsibility, but we may also lose an emphasis on prayer, discernment, and compassion. When we strive for higher numbers, using a marketing approach, we may get many people in our pews (or stadium seats), but we may also find that we're constantly trying to create "church-a-palooza," focusing more and more on entertainment. Even when striving to be more missional, we can end up focusing so much on efforts beyond our walls that we forget about the need to pay attention to what is happening within our walls.

Ultimately, what we strive for is what we get. At the core of any church there needs to be a striving for God. Without an understanding that the church is primarily about helping people connect with, experience, and be grounded in God, everything else crumbles. If we strive first for the kingdom of God, then we become a church that accomplishes what the other models try to achieve: empowering people, being fiscally responsible in a God-led way, creating experiences that lead people to encounter God, and developing a passion for mission.

Striving for God opens up everything else. But if we strive for everything else, we may never really open up to God.

Proverb 40.

If we merely seek leaders with good organizing,
teaching, accounting, or property skills, why then
complain that our members are uninspired?
If we seek leaders with a yearning for God,
they will lead others to be inspired.

MOST CHURCHES, WHEN SEEKING NEW LEADERS to fill leadership positions on their boards and committees, do what's typically done in corporations, businesses, and organizations: look for the person with the skills to get the job done. Makes sense. Why would we want to fill these positions with someone who is incompetent—who can't get the job done?

So, when looking for someone to oversee the church building, we get someone who is good at building-type stuff. When looking for someone to oversee the budgets and finances, we look for someone with an accounting or bookkeeping background. When looking for someone to lead our education programs, we look for someone who had a background and skills in education or child development.

This approach makes so much sense, if our goal is trying to staff a business or a community board. But we're not. What makes churches distinct from every other entity is that our focus is primarily spiritual and relational, not organizational. We are trying to create a place where people yearn to follow Christ. We are trying to create a place where people experience the Holy Spirit. We are trying to create a place that helps them discern their calling and discover their purpose. If that's our primary purpose, why do we consistently lift up leaders whose primary skills are the functional, not the spiritual? Their functional skills may be good if the church needs to replace the

111

roof, recruit new teachers, or analyze the balance sheet. Yet what if the issue to decide is embarking on a new mission to put aside funds to help those being evicted from their homes? What if the issue is whether or not to renovate a sanctuary or change musical directions in worship? What if the issue is supporting a new church development in an impoverished area?

Do we really want the people making these decisions to base their decisions on the bottom line, on what we can afford, or on what bad things might happen if we commit ourselves and then fail? When taking the step to follow where God is calling, don't we want leaders who are passionate about following God's calling?

The primary question, when raising up leaders, should be something similar to what we find in the book of Acts. The apostles were spending as much time distributing food as they were teaching and preaching, so they decided to lift up new leaders whose focus would be mainly on distributing the food. What were the qualifications they looked for? If they were part of the modern church, they would have looked for people with experience in logistics, food prep, or who had worked before in the church kitchen. That's not what the apostles looked for. Their job description ran like this: "Therefore, friends, select from among yourselves seven men of good standing, full of the Spirit and of wisdom, whom we may appoint to this task, while we, for our part, will devote ourselves to prayer and to serving the word" (Acts 6:3–4). The personal qualities they looked for were being of good standing, being full of the Spirit, and having wisdom.

They sought people to serve food, but who also could lead people to God. They chose other leaders in ministry and mission who understood that the primary focus was a yearning for God.

Too many of our churches lift up leaders who may not have much of a passion for God. For example, a number of years ago, while I was leading a workshop on church transformation, a pastor stood up and asked a question: "I hear what you are saying about lifting up spiritual leaders. My question is what I should do with my board. We've tried to be as inclusive as possible, so what do I tell my two elders who are also atheists?"

I wasn't quite sure how to answer, other than to laugh. I finally said something akin to, "I appreciate the need to be inclusive of others, especially of atheists. But why would you put someone who fundamentally doesn't believe in God in a position of leading people to experience God?" The pastor replied, "Huh! I never thought of it that way before."

Who we raise up to lead us will lead us where they are most comfortable. If they are comfortable with seeking God, they will lead others in the search for God. If they aren't comfortable seeking God, then the church won't be, either.

Proverb 41.

If a congregation is whining like a bunch of babies,
it usually means that we need to let them
take baby steps.

M ANY CONGREGATIONS WHINE when new pastors come in and start implementing the changes those churches said that they wanted before the pastor came. This whining can be the bane of many pastors' existence and the subject of their own subsequent whining.

Too often pastors share a common complaint about their congregations: "They said they wanted to change. They said they wanted to grow. But when I started doing what they said they wanted, all they did was complain. Why did they lie to me?" They didn't lie. They really did want change. They just weren't ready for the pace of change.

Chip and Dan Heath, authors of the groundbreaking book *Made to Stick*, cited earlier, identify the problem. They say that the problem is "the curse of knowledge."[1] What's the curse of knowledge? It's the reality that as we gain expertise in any field, we develop so much knowledge that we no longer remember what it was like before we had that knowledge. And so we lose our sensitivity to those who don't have our knowledge.

All mainline church pastors have gone to seminary. Most have spent at least three years gaining expertise in scripture, theology, church dynamics, and (hopefully) spiritual practices. Then, when they go into a church, they read books on church growth and leadership. And they go to workshops and conferences on growing their churches. They gain great knowledge.

---

1. Heath and Heath, *Made to Stick*, Kindle edition, location 312 of 5195.

Meanwhile, the members of their congregations didn't go to seminary. They never read those books. They never attended those workshops and conferences. So, when we enthusiastically implement changes, our members don't always understand the changes, the reasons for the changes, nor the need to have so many changes so quickly. That's why they whine like babies. They've not been blessed with our knowledge, and our blessing turns into our curse.

Just as we would never demand that infants walk before they can crawl, or run before they can walk, demanding that churches change at our pace creates anxiety and turmoil. They called us because they wanted our expertise, but that doesn't mean that they have our expertise. They aren't babies. They just lack knowledge and experience.

When we experience our churches as whining like babies, we need to resist whining like babies in response. Instead, we need to recognize that what seems like one small step for us is one giant leap for our members. So break down those steps. Slow the changes down. Have some patience. Try to remember your own knowledge before going to seminary, reading those books, or attending those workshops. Make the changes, but make the steps smaller so that your members can gain confidence and faith.

If you are going to add more contemporary music to a traditional worship service, start by adding one song per service for a while to get them used to it. After they get used to those songs, you can increase their frequency. If you want your church to engage more in mission, start with smaller missions that help them grow in confidence, and then build up to bigger and more complex missions. If you want them to be more welcoming, work on training a few members in being more welcoming, and then let them teach the congregation to become more welcoming.

Criticizing them isn't going to get them to follow more willingly. You wouldn't criticize or berate an infant for not being a child, a child for not being a teen, a teen for not being an adult. . . . Well, we do berate teens for not being adults, but you get my point. You would recognize where they are in their maturity, and then help them slowly become more mature.

So, when we whine like babies because our congregations are whining like a bunch of babies, recognize that we need to help them take baby steps so that they can eventually make giant leaps.

Proverb 42.

Too often pastors become disappointed because their churches aren't more mature. But if their churches were more mature, they wouldn't need a pastor. So pastors need to remember that their role is to lead churches to maturity, just as a parent's role is to lead children to maturity.

I N MY WORK AS A SPIRITUAL DIRECTOR, counselor, and mentor with pastors, I've often heard the same complaint about their churches: "They said they wanted to grow. They said that they wanted to change. They said that they were ready for something new. But now that I'm offering that, all they do is whine, snipe, bitch, and moan." They are basically complaining that the leaders and members of the church, who seemed so mature during initial interviews and subsequent conversations, now seem so immature in dealing with change. How did the church get so immature?

It's not that the church became immature. The church just was what it was. The truth is that if the church was a fully mature, deeply spiritual, wonderfully Spirit-filled church, it wouldn't need a pastor. A pastor's role is to shepherd a church to a deeper spiritual, relational, and missional maturity. When the church whines, snipes, and complains, it simply reveals that the church lacks maturity and needs the guidance of a mature pastor. Don't we want a church that needs us?

Is there really any difference between the way our churches act and the way the disciples acted with Jesus? From what I can tell, they were constantly acting like children. They constantly misunderstood Jesus's message just as some people misinterpret our sermons. They constantly acted out of jealousy when one disciple got closer to Jesus than the others, just as some members complain that we pastors play favoritism. They vied for power in Jesus's upcoming kingdom, just as members can vie for position and power in our churches. They betrayed, denied, and ran away from Jesus. Has that ever happened to any of us as pastors or church leaders? But they also eventually became deeply mature.

Our calling as church leaders is to primarily work on our own spiritual, psychological, and relational maturity so that we can lead others to it because we can't lead them where we've never been. We don't have to be perfect, but we do have to work on it. Just as immature parents can't effectively parent children, so immature pastors can't effectively lead churches.

As we work on our own maturity, we have to recognize that spiritual immaturity is normal for people who haven't really grown. We don't lambast our five year olds for not being twenty-one. We recognize that growth takes time. The same thing is often true for our churches.

So when our churches lack maturity, the best response is to patiently help them grow, while we work on our own maturity.

Proverb 43.

*Just because someone says something offensive
to us doesn't mean we have to be offended.
Just because someone rejects us doesn't mean we
have to reject her or him. Treating people in kind
generally makes us less kind. Being a leader means
treating people better than they treat us in order
to help them become better people.*

A REALITY OF MINISTRY IS THAT PEOPLE will say offensive things to us. They don't mean to, but they do it anyway. I've had my share of really ignorant things said to me. Here are some of my greatest offensive hits: "Pastor, why did you preach that sermon on a communion Sunday?" "You've certainly gained a lot of weight since the last time I visited here." "Hmmm, I thought a person of your reputation would preach a much better sermon than what I just heard." "That story you told on Sunday ruined Easter for me and my whole family." How do we respond to comments like these?

We also will be rejected. No matter how skilled we are as pastors, or as church leaders, people who leave us to join other churches will reject us. That's fine as long as we never see them again, but what do we do when we see them in a grocery store, at a high school graduation, or in a restaurant? Do we reject them in return?

I remember a conversation I had with a relatively new church member. Her family had joined our church from another church in town. They liked their old church, but they struggled with the new pastor's constant preaching about who was or wasn't saved. His sermons felt too much like judgment against everyone. After visiting every other church in town, they decided to join our church. Soon afterward the wife of the previous church's pastor called the mother and said, "How could you do this to us? After all the ways we've supported you? You've turned your back on us! You ARE NOT being a Christian. And you've hurt my husband terribly!" She felt rejected because the pastor felt rejected, and so she was calling to reject the rejecter. Just because we've been rejected doesn't mean we have to reject.

As church leaders, we are called to rise above all of the offensive, rejecting, ignorant, and hurtful things said to us. We don't have to respond in kind. Why are people so ignorant to us? Because "they do not know what they are doing" (Luke 23:34). We are called to follow Christ, who says, "But I say to you, Love your enemies and pray for those who persecute you, so that you may be children of your Father in heaven" (Matthew 5:44–45).

If we see someone in a restaurant who has walked away from our church, are we willing to show that person that we still care about him by greeting and talking with him? We don't have to talk about why he left. All we need to do is to show we care. If someone says something offensive, can we let it go? Saying something offensive in return only increases defensiveness on her part and ours. There are times when we may need to defend ourselves, but not because we are offended. And when we do defend ourselves, we need to do so in a way that doesn't attack in return.

When someone says something offensive to us, we don't have to be offended and become defensive. We can respond by letting it slide by, making light of the comment, or simply saying to him, "I'm sorry." If someone rejects us, we can still love her. Perhaps not more closely, but we can still show her that we will not treat her in kind, and that we will respond with kindness.

Proverb 44.

When people say they are "spiritual but not religious," they are rightly telling the church that we are "religious but not spiritual." The answer for both is to become spiritual and religious.

W E LIVE IN INDIVIDUALISTIC TIMES—times in which the pursuit of individuality is always praised above the community. People shy away from commitments and they distrust institutions, while a significant portion of our population spends their lives trying to stand out from the crowd in one way or another.

This pursuit of individuality would have been baffling in ancient times. In biblical times, the community was always more important than the individual. People derived their identities from their families, their villages, and their religion. They derived their identities from who they came from, not what they did. They didn't see themselves as distinct persons living in communities. They saw themselves as extensions of the family and the community.

Perhaps they were too communal in those days. Just as in modern Middle Eastern culture, where people focus too much on family honor, shaming, and sometimes ostracizing, ancient people lost themselves in their communities, to the detriment of their individuality. What was really radical about the early Christian faith was that it lifted up the individual so that every person mattered. Over the centuries Christian culture has struggled to care about each person. But we've swung so far in the direction of individuality that we now worship individuality, while losing the spiritual centrality of community.

We idolize individuals who have seemingly risen out of the pool of commonality. We revere film and television stars, pop stars, American Idols, professional athletes, billionaires, and anyone who can tangibly celebrate his or her success of individuality over common communality.

This modern emphasis of "me" over "we" has given life to the belief that we can be "spiritual but not religious." It has given life to the belief that we can form a vibrant spirituality by picking and choosing from among all the different religious traditions. The "spiritual but not religious" treat spirituality like a Sunday brunch. Brunch isn't very healthy, but it's awfully good as we pile on our plates a bacon and cheese omelet, pancakes, brownies, hash browns, waffles, bacon, sausage, cookies, and a few more tasty treats. In their spiritual brunch they choose a God omelet filled with Jesus and Buddha, and then grab a bowl of yoga, a Daoist pancake topped with Native American dream catchers, Muslim hash browns, and a cookie cake of self-created ideas and rituals.

The irony is that they don't dabble in the one thing that all of those faiths have in common—an emphasis on community. Not one of those faith traditions has raised the individual above the communal, even if Christianity did recognize the importance of the individual. All see the individual as part of the communal. This means that being "spiritual but not religious" can actually make us not very spiritual because we reject the community that is part of a vibrant spirituality.

Still, we have to listen to those who claim to be "spiritual but not religious" because they are making a valid point about our churches. Implied in their phrase is the reality that too many of our modern churches are "religious but not spiritual." A significant reason these people say that they are "spiritual but not religious" is their recognition that most churches, and even denominations, have chosen to emphasize the religious and theological over the spiritual.

A significant number of today's churches emphasize biblical knowledge, theological creeds and confessions, doctrine and dogma, and religious rituals. But they don't connect them to a vibrant spiritual life. Basically, some act as though just showing up for church or mass on Sundays gets us into heaven when we die. Or as if knowing the Bible well enough, or having the right theology, will get God to bless us with lots of "bling." Or as if singing the right hymns or songs, going to the right church, listening to the right preacher, and/or confessing in the "right" way our faith in Jesus Christ will make us saved.

Many people outside of our churches aren't looking for salvation or justification. They are looking for connection. They want to experience God, the Divine, which they experience periodically by walking in the woods, hiking up a mountain, standing by a lakeshore, in their yoga class, meditation class, or by reading Eckhart Tolle's latest book.

What they are telling us is that they no longer feel like we help them connect with God. How often do we hear this criticism? How often do we pay attention to this criticism? Mostly we criticize them, calling them shallow and religion-lite. But we need to hear them.

We need to hear them enough to seriously consider how to make our churches both spiritual *and* religious. Do we need to transform our rituals, our preaching, our music, our teachings, and our structure in a way that helps people become part of a genuine spiritual community? Do we need to renew our churches in a way that helps people develop a vibrant spirituality?

The first step may be for us, as Christians, to recapture a vibrant spirituality for ourselves that reinvigorates our theological thinking and our religious practice in our communities.

Proverb 45.

When we get caught up in the darkness of life, we generally only notice God's absence. But when we look for light, we discover God's presence. Lead people to look for light, especially in darkness.

THERE'S A COMMON CULTURAL BELIEF about the way God works that's both persistent and pernicious. It's summed up in the oft-said phrase, "If God is such a good god, then why does God let bad things happened to good people?" This is the lament of so many people who've walked away from God. It expresses a belief that if we are good, God should only allow good to happen to us. If we are bad, then bad should happen to us. Since most people see themselves as basically good, they believe that they should be immune to tragedy, sorrow, death, devastation, the breakup of relationships, being fired from a job, getting a significant illness, and so much more.

The irony is that there's virtually nothing in the Bible suggesting that God allows good people to experience only good things. In fact, the Bible suggests that if we are truly good, we may experience more bad than we would anticipate because acts of goodness in the world often spawn bad responses. And because we are called to good especially amidst the bad.

There's no good figure in the Bible who doesn't experience the struggles of life. Noah is given a seemingly impossible and ridiculous task of building the ark. He is mocked and derided by everyone. And after the flood, it is just he and his family. He has to struggle to rebuild his life and the world amidst his loneliness. Abraham is called out of a comfortable life in the city to struggle as a nomad in the wilderness. He experiences all sorts of struggles and turmoil. Joseph becomes a slave and a prisoner. Moses lives for forty years in the desert, and then leads the Israelites for another forty years in the desert. Job loses everything as a test of his faith. David, after his anoint-ment as king, spends twelve years as an outlaw being chased by the murderous King Saul. The prophets are mocked and mistreated. The northern kingdom of Israel is defeated and dispersed. The Jewish people of Judah are made slaves in Bab-ylon for seventy years. Jesus is crucified. The apostles spread the word, and are mocked, flogged, imprisoned, and killed for their efforts.

To be a good person in the Bible means to spread God's light in the world's darkness. Good people aren't automati-cally given good things. In fact they are often called to be good to the bad, or at least to those that have flirted with badness. The one really clear thing about good people—people who are good in faith—is that they see blessings and grace especially in dark and difficult times. They are light in the darkness.

As churches and church leaders, we are called to be that light in the darkness. We are called to help people immersed in darkness discover God's light. But we can't do that if we only see what's wrong in life. For example, if all we do is com-plain about the degradation of society, the sinfulness of peo-ple, and all of society's woes—racism, poverty, immorality, the proliferation of drugs and addictive substances, those people we see as bad and reprehensible, the government, business, and everything else—we become part of the darkness. We can point them out, but even more we need to point people to the light—to become light.

The responsibility of leaders is to nurture a culture and community of light that leads people to experience God's goodness especially in dark times.

Proverb 46.

Remember that no matter how much the dogs bark,
the mail gets delivered anyway. Learn to distinguish
between the members who bark and those who bite.

P EOPLE LIKE TO COMPLAIN. They especially like to complain about change. We all like some sort of stability,
while at the same time we still like surprises. We're a
funny bunch. We want things to stay the same, but we also
like it when something stirs up the sameness, making it different. We just don't like it when the mixing spoon digs too
deeply into our lives, churning everything up.

All people resist change, and the more change they anticipate, the more they resist. All counselors and therapists recognize this dynamic. They're all trained to understand defense
mechanisms, but they're also trained to understand that
before a defense mechanism is deployed, small acts of resistance precede.

Resistance isn't full-blown defense. It's milder and more
tentative. A good therapist doesn't try to pull down a person's
defenses because that only makes the person more defensive.
A good therapist works on helping the person recognize and
let go of her resistance before she becomes defensive.

So what is resistance? It's barking dogs. Whenever someone steps on our property, friend or foe, our dogs bark. That's
not the same as saying that they bite. Our thirteen-pound
dog barks ferociously every time the UPS deliveryman drops
something at our doorstep, but she would rather play with
him than bite him. Her bark is ferocious, but it's especially so
because of what she's noticed: whenever she barks, he eventually turns around, gets back in his truck, and drives away. She
thinks it's because of her. Yet all that barking doesn't stop him

from leaving a package. She doesn't realize it, but her barking really isn't all that powerful because she doesn't bite, and even if she could, she doesn't get the opportunity.

Barking is resistance. It's an attempt at defense. Whenever we, as leaders, spearhead some sort of change, people will bark. The reason is that they've learned from the past that if they make enough noise, pastors and leaders will get scared and back off. Good leaders can tell the difference between the sounds of barking and the threats of biting. Good leaders don't ignore the barking, but they don't give it more power than it deserves. They deliver anyway.

Being barked at by members when leading a congregation into change is part of the job. It's simply the noise of resistance a church makes when it isn't quite sure if it's ready to move forward. Our job is to determine if this is just barking or really a prelude to biting. If we sense that people are just barking, we need to move forward gently despite the racket. We need to lead the change. On the other hand, if we realize that the barking is about to turn into biting, that the resistance is now turning into potentially damaging defensiveness, we need to back off and help people feel more secure with the anticipated change.

A biting dog, under the guidance of a good dog trainer, can be tamed enough to bark but not bite. He does it by recognizing that most biting dogs are fearful, defensive dogs. So he helps the dog feel safe in the face of whatever is going on around it. The dog most likely to bite is the dog that's most afraid and feels the least secure.

So with churches, defensive church members will feel like they are part of the process when they feel safe and cared about. The point isn't to let biting members stop us. Instead, it is to pay attention to those who bite and help them feel safe so that they can be part of the church's movement forward.

Proverb 47.

*How we make decisions is much more important
than what decisions we make. When decisions
are made communally, respectfully, and prayerfully,
they lead us to serve God. When they aren't,
even the best decisions can be divisive.*

I'VE OFTEN BEEN FASCINATED by the different decisions churches make, wondering if God is secretly only on one side, or if God can be on both sides, of an issue. For example, does God value the decisions made by more progressive churches because God is a progressive, or by more conservative churches because God is a conservative? Does God bless one kind of church over the other because it happened upon the right kinds of ministries and missions, or does God bless all ministries and missions, even though they may be denominationally and politically opposed to each other?

With the proliferation of so many different churches, with so many different perspectives, theological beliefs, and historical traditions, how do we know which decisions are really the ones God wants, and which ones aren't? Is it based on the size of the church? By the amount of money devoted to a ministry or mission? By how happy or angry the church is over the decision? There certainly are an awful lot of Christians out there who are convinced that God is only on their side because . . . well . . . they're just RIGHT.

With so many different churches seeking God in so many different ways, what's the criteria God uses to determine which efforts to bless or not? I could never ultimately determine which churches God blesses more and which less, but I can certainly tell what decisions *seem* to be blessed the most. It's the decisions that fulfill the teachings of Paul: "I therefore, the prisoner in the Lord, beg you to lead a life worthy of the calling to which you have been called, with all humility and gentleness, with patience, bearing with one another in love, making every effort to maintain the unity of the Spirit in the bond of peace" (Ephesians 4:1–3).

He also says, "If then there is any encouragement in Christ, any consolation from love, any sharing in the Spirit, any compassion and sympathy, make my joy complete: be of the same mind, having the same love, being in full accord and of one mind. Do nothing from selfish ambition or conceit, but in humility regard others as better than yourselves. Let each of you look not to your own interests, but to the interests of others. Let the same mind be in you that was in Christ Jesus" (Philippians 2:1–5).

Finally, he says, "As God's chosen ones, holy and beloved, clothe yourselves with compassion, kindness, humility, meekness, and patience. Bear with one another and, if anyone has a complaint against another, forgive each other; just as the Lord has forgiven you, so you also must forgive. Above all, clothe yourselves with love, which binds everything together in perfect harmony. And let the peace of Christ rule in your hearts, to which indeed you were called in the one body. And be thankful" (Colossians 3:12–15).

From Paul's perspective it seems to matter more *how* we make decisions rather than *what* decisions we make. If we make decisions together, with humility, really listening to and integrating other people's perspectives, while bearing each other's burdens, then we will be making God-instilled decisions that will be filled with God's blessings.

The reality of most churches, though, is that they tend to make decisions on a majority-rules basis. For them it doesn't matter how the decisions are made. What matters is that we follow the majority because God *must* be on the side of the majority. It's no surprise, then, that in so many churches the decisions they make are divisive and lead to losses in the church.

Decisions are often made with a sense of superiority, whether those decisions have to do with the issues surrounding homosexuality or the color of paint used to paint the church hall.

For the most part it's apparent that God cares more about *how* we make decisions than *what* decisions we make. That doesn't mean that any decision is blessed, no matter how bad the decision is, as long as the decision is made harmoniously. Nor that God doesn't care about our decisions if they aren't harmoniously made. If the decision is destructive, even if it is unanimous, then it's hard to imagine that it garners God's full blessing.

Good pastoral and church leaders know how to help people make decisions together in a way that brings people together. They know how to help people make decisions that are humble, loving, that bind people together, that bear with one another, maintain the unity of the Spirit, and create bonds of peace. Usually these leaders lead people to these kinds of decisions because these leaders have these qualities in themselves.

Proverb 48.

*Every ministry has a lifespan. When we force
dying ministries to stay alive, we also prevent new
ministries from being resurrected from their death.
Learn to let ministries and missions die when
they need to, so that new ministries and missions
can be born in their place.*

A MAJOR PROBLEM OF ANY STRUGGLING CHURCH is that it consistently does what it's always done before, and avoids doing what it's never done before. Whenever a church has maintained a long-term ministry or mission—one that started with such passion, and that sustained energy for a long time—the ministry will eventually go into decline. It's inevitable. We talked about this in Proverb 30. It's the problem of entropy. Every church, every ministry, every pastor, and every leader eventually declines.

Decline isn't the issue. Allowing things to die is. If there's no death, there's no resurrection. And without resurrection, there's no new life. There's a life cycle for everything: "For everything there is a season, and a time for every matter under heaven: a time to be born, and a time to die; a time to plant, and a time to pluck up what is planted" (Ecclesiastes 3:1–2).

Ecclesiastes speaks an eternal truth, but we try to prevent it by never letting anything die, nor by plucking up what is planted. We often just keep doing the same old ministries that were done in the 1980s. We often just keep playing the same music that was played in the 1960s. We often just keep reading the same books, doing the same fundraisers, preaching the same sermons, reading the same materials, and engaging in the same mission programs that have been done before, year after year—especially after people have stopped responding to

131

them. Keeping things alive that need to die can keep us from being creative.

It can be really hard to let certain ministries and missions go, but good leadership knows when to give people permission to let go. For example, when I first came to Calvin Presbyterian Church, I got to see the wonderful Easter Sunrise Service that the church had been doing for years. The youth group led it, and it had a wonderful combination of depth and humor. Each year the worshippers included members of the youth group, their families, and a few other church members.

The following year the youth director, who also happened to be our music director, asked me if they had to keep doing the sunrise service. I asked him what the problem was. He said, "It's mostly just the youth and their families that come, but it also makes it really hard for me to prepare for the regular Easter service. I spend so much time corralling the teens, making sure they're organized, that I don't really get to do much that's creative in the regular Easter service."

I immediately said to him, "Yeah, go ahead. Don't do it. We'll make sure the Worship Committee knows." He replied, "What are you going to do with the people who complain?" I said, "I'll invite them to organize it next year." And that's what happened. We had an older member complain that we weren't doing the sunrise service, which was her favorite service. I invited her to organize it. She said, "Well, I don't like it *that* much."

We needed to let the service die for something else to come alive. The following year we added an earlier service to our normal Sunday morning routine because of the church's growth, which made organizing for those two services harder. To still have had a sunrise service would have made Easter Sunday really stressful for the worship staff. We had to let the sunrise service die so that we could become more creative for our regular two Easter services.

Letting ministries and missions die at the appropriate time allows new ministries and missions to be born and thrive. A way of thinking about this is by looking at the number of original Christian churches that still exist. Do you know the answer? The answer is none. Even those original churches died so that new ones could be born. And Christianity has been experiencing the cycle of birth, death, resurrection, new birth, life, death, resurrection ever since.

Proverb 49.

Never work harder than our members. If we do,
they'll let us do all the work.

ANY YEARS AGO WHEN I WAS A THERAPIST, I had a young patient I was trying to help overcome his grief. His older sister had died of a drug overdose. Before she died, she had told him that if he didn't let her go in his heart, she wouldn't really die. He took what she said literally, thinking that if he denied her death at some level, she would find a way to come back to life.

I worked hard with that patient. It wasn't easy. We spent a lot of time talking about his feelings surrounding her death. We even had a counseling session on her grave. What made the sessions difficult was that he wasn't much of a talker. He would give me one- and two-word answers to my questions. It was frustrating because he broke my heart. I wanted so much to help him move beyond his grief, but he seemed stalled.

Eventually I went to my supervisor for help. He suggested we videotape a session so that he could observe what I was doing. So we did. After watching for ten minutes, he said to me, "Wow! You're working really hard. I've rarely seen a therapist work so hard with a patient." My pride swelled when he said that. I thought, "Yes, I may be the hardest-working therapist ever." Then he said, "You know, if you keep working that hard, he'll never get better. You're doing all the work for him. Why should he work on himself when you'll do it for him? Never work harder than your patients. If you do, they'll let you do all the work and they'll never get better."

I took that to heart then, and I take it to heart now in ministry. As pastors and leaders, if we do all the work in the church, the church will never grow in ministry, mission, or membership. Part of good leadership is leading in a way that makes it feel almost as if the leader isn't necessary for the church to operate. Good leaders delegate work, but do so in a way that makes clear what the work is. The pastor can't be expected to do all the work in setting the church's course, attending and guiding the board and committees, visiting hospitalized and homebound, being involved in all the mission projects, teaching classes, leading youth groups, and preaching sermons. It's too much work for one or two or many people, but it also doesn't create space for members to do the work of the church.

Here's the rub, though. When I backed off with my patient and let him do the work, we ended up with a number of sessions where there were long, painful periods of silence. He wasn't quite ready to jump into the breach and work harder. I had to create the space for him to eventually work harder, and that took a while.

For churches, the same dynamic occurs. Just because we step back doesn't mean that everyone will rush forward. It takes time. Good leadership invites people into ministry and mission, but it also patiently waits (sometimes for years) for people to step forward to do the work. The key is that until we step back, they can't step forward.

Proverb 50.

Just because we are certain doesn't make us right,
but it certainly can make us self-righteous.

ELF-RIGHTEOUSNESS IS AN ATTITUDE that plagues many pastors and church leaders. As a result it plagues many churches. Unfortunately, most self-righteous people are so certain that they are right that they can't see how self-righteous they are.

Self-righteousness doesn't come from being right. It comes from being certain. My wife's Irish Catholic family has an unofficial motto that I love, and it applies to so many people in life: "Often in error; never in doubt." Self-righteous people never allow their errors to interfere with their certainty. And that certainty can lead to negativity and disunity, especially when that certainty is based on faulty beliefs.

The best leaders lead out of the sense of humility. Unfortunately, too many people inside and outside the church don't understand what real humility is. Humility isn't weakness. It isn't fearfulness and trepidation. It doesn't seek peace and avoid conflict. It doesn't focus on letting people have their way.

Real humility is the awareness that only God matters, and that we are committed to seeking and doing what God is calling us to do above everything else. Humility means adopting an attitude that God is speaking to us constantly through everything. It means taking on an approach to everything that says to God, "I am available to you right now to do your will."

Humility in leadership means never being certain, but moving forward confidently with God—confidence literally means "to have faith with"—once we have a sense of a calling from God. Don't mistake this confidence with arrogance. To be a humble leader means moving forward with confidence, and leading others to move forward with confidence, on a path we've sensed God is leading us on. Amidst that confidence we are always humble enough to reconsider the path if we eventually sense that we've discerned incorrectly. We don't move forward with certainty, but with humility, and that willingness to let go of a need for certainty gives us great availability to God. Humble leaders don't become self-righteous because they are neither overly concerned with self, nor with being "right."

To be a humble leader means to be a prayerful leader who puts discernment of God's will at the forefront of her or his leadership. Humble leaders don't care about certainty; they care about discerning a path and leading others on that path.

Too many church leaders lead churches to make decisions based on their own self-righteousness. This seems to be true of self-righteous leaders on both the left and the right who are so certain that they are right about whatever cultural issues swirl around the church. They can whip their members into a frenzy of outrage over this issue or that. But when they are that self-righteous, they lose sight of God's will. Perhaps God does want them to take a stand, but in a way that is filled with the fruits of the spirit: "love, joy, peace, patience, kindness, generosity, faithfulness, gentleness, and self-control" (Galatians 5:22).

Leading people down God's path means leading in a way that is humbly aware of God's call; that is prayerful enough to seek God's call; that is courageous enough to follow God's call; and that is selfless enough to go back and reconsider all the time whether or not they are still following God's call. It is not the path of certainty. It is the path of humble availability.

Proverb 51.

We never regret a wise decision, but we
always regret the selfish one.

THERE ARE SEVERAL CHRISTIAN WORDS that don't get used much in modern Christianity. We don't talk much about "humility" anymore, even though humility is very much part of the Gospel message. There are reasons we don't talk about humility much. It seems to conflict with Western democratic and capitalistic values that emphasize strength; and humility seems like weakness.

We don't talk much about "denying self," even if Jesus constantly reminds people to pick up their crosses, deny themselves, and follow him (Matthew 16:24). We live in a culture that emphasizes self-promotion. So self-denial seems to move in the wrong direction.

Another word that's not used much anymore is "wisdom." We seek expediency, efficiency, and effectiveness in our decision making, but not wisdom. We make decisions that serve our own interests, but not necessarily those that are wise. What is wisdom?

Wisdom is incredibly hard to define, although a number of books of the Bible, including Proverbs, are devoted to it. Ultimately, wisdom is the attempt to tap into God's mind rather than just our own. It is a spiritual undertaking rather than a rational one. Wisdom emerges out of our openness to the Spirit, and a conforming of our minds to Christ's mind: "And the Holy Spirit also testifies to us, for after saying, 'This is the covenant that I will make with them after those days, says the Lord: I will put my laws in their hearts, and I will write them on their minds'" (Hebrews 10:15–16). We attempt to live out of God's will discerned in our hearts, rather than the pure reasonings of our minds.

The difficulty is that it is very difficult to determine what is of God's mind, and what is just our own ego masquerading as God's mind. The key is determining whether what we are deciding is for ourselves or for others. God leads us to make decisions that are best for others, but not necessarily for ourselves. We tend to make decisions that are best for ourselves, but not always with others in mind. The decisions may be mutually beneficial, but the focus is still on self.

When leading people to make decisions, those that are steeped in a genuine desire for wisdom tend to build up and unite people. Those decisions that are made for self-focused reasons (because someone has an agenda, because a group of people want a particular outcome, or because one or more think it would be the "best idea") all tend to be regretted later. Wise decisions are rarely regretted.

Good leadership seeks wisdom.

Proverb 52.

If the church can't live without us, then it's
probably on its way to dying with us.

MOST OF US WANT TO BE INDISPENSABLE. Most of us want to be needed. One of the worst feelings in the world comes at that moment when we realize our children don't really need us as much anymore. A struggle in marriages comes when we sense that our spouse really doesn't need us much, whether or not that sense is accurate. As leaders, and especially as pastors, sensing that we are being taken for granted by our members is a really bad feeling. But good leaders are always being taken for granted because they lead in a way that makes them seem like they aren't needed.

Seeming like they aren't needed is not the same as not being needed. The two are drastically different. Good leaders are always necessary and needed. It's just that they lead in a way that doesn't seem like they are necessary and needed. They don't seem necessary and needed because they are good at setting a course and direction that moves toward a particular vision. They are good at articulating that vision in a way that people can easily grasp and embrace for themselves. They are good at helping people understand the large and small steps that move the church in that direction. And they are good at letting people walk the path themselves.

Good leaders step in periodically to help people stay on course. They also help those who are lost, or moving in a counter-productive direction, find their way back. But they are also content to step back and let the members find their own way. While they are doing that, the good leaders are often exploring ahead, developing themselves so that when the next challenge emerges, they are ready to help the church overcome it.

Still, good leaders don't make themselves indispensable because if they are indispensable the church cannot function without them. The mark of a good leader is that if the leader leaves, the church is sad, it wishes her or him well, and it keeps operating at a fairly high level. If the pastor is indispensable to the church, then it probably was on a dying course anyway. They were being treated like babies who could not be trusted to make their own decisions and follow the path themselves.

To be personally indispensable means to make God dispensable, and if God becomes dispensable in a church, then the church is on its way to become disposable.

Proverb 53.

Whether we like it or not, pastors are often expected to be the most mature persons in a room, which means that other leaders may treat us poorly while treating problem people well. Pastors have to learn how to respond to the most painful situations in spiritually mature ways.

Y EARS AGO, WHILE GIVING A TALK IN CANADA to a large group of pastors and church leaders, a teary-eyed pastor stood up to ask a question as she challenged me on a comment. She said that in the previous few years she had gone through very tough times. She had gone through a divorce, which also meant going through financial difficulties. What disturbed her most was the fact that her church didn't step up to minister to her. Members rarely called to ask her how she was. No one brought meals to her. Some sent notes of support, but not enough. When members of the church went through similar struggles, the church had supported them in such ways. She had tried to leave and find another church, but nothing ever became available. She asked me how to be an effective pastor when it seemed like no one in her congregation cared about her.

How do you answer a question like that? It's not only a tough question to answer, but it's fraught with danger. If I didn't answer how she wanted, which really was to support her in her pain, then I could be the target of her hurt. At the same time, is her role in a church to be ministered to if she is a minister?

I took a deep breath and told her that I understood her pain, but that she didn't fully understand her role. To be a pastor means to be the most mature person in the room, and that means having the ability to care about others when they don't really show that they care about us. In many ways, it's like being a parent to children. How many of us would complain that our children don't parent us? How many of us would complain that our teens don't take care of us? We may complain that our kids don't appreciate us, but that's just the typical parental venting. We don't expect our kids to be our parents.

Pastors are expected to be the most mature people in the room. It's for this reason that when there is conflict in a church between the pastor and a completely unreasonable person, the church may inexplicably choose to side with the unreasonable person. I've worked with several pastors who've experienced this dynamic. They've had conflict with an unreasonable staff member or powerful church figure. But the church board didn't come down on the unreasonable person. They tried to get help for the pastor in dealing with the conflict by suggesting counseling or conflict resolution workshops. So, were they really siding with the unreasonable person?

My sense is that the boards knew that the unreasonable person was unreasonable. They also knew that the unreasonable person had little or no maturity, and that she or he wasn't going to change no matter how they might intervene. So they tried to manage the pastor instead. They figured that the pastor was mature enough to deal with the pain, but they knew that the unreasonable person wasn't. So they did what they could to placate the unreasonable person, while never really saying to the pastor, "I support you and think you're right."

This tradition of expecting pastors to be the most mature person in the room is very much part of the Book of Acts. The apostles and evangelists always positioned themselves as the most spiritually mature people in the room and the region. They were willing to be falsely accused, flogged, falsely imprisoned, maligned, and ignored, but it didn't stop them from serving Christ. In this they were imitating Christ, who was always the most mature person in the room.

Our task as leaders, and especially pastoral leaders, is to have high expectations for ourselves to always lead with maturity. This means that if we are struggling, we may need to get counseling. We may need spiritual direction. We may need coaching. We may need training. We may need to find friends outside of the church who can lift us up when we are down. It means that pastors themselves need to find friends among other pastors (which can be hard in some denominations where pastors can act more like enemies as they try to weed out the heretics). It means that pastors and other leaders need to do what they can to become more spiritually, psychologically, relationally, and professionally mature. The alternative is that if we don't gain maturity, we won't be able to lead others to maturity—a maturity that is able to offer support to people in pain.

Proverb 54.

Visionary leaders see the horizon, figure out how to get there, and forge a path for others. Ordinary leaders either only see the path and get lost, or only point to the horizon while going nowhere.

E VERY CHURCH WANTS THEIR PASTOR to be a visionary leader. At least that's what churches searching for new pastors seem to say. They want someone who has a vision and knows how to accomplish that vision. So what is vision?

Vision is the ability to see the horizon, to point to that horizon with passion so that others can clearly see it (like asking them to see a far off mountain), and then helping them take the steps to get there.

It's difficult to be truly visionary because it requires looking into the distance while at the same time guiding people to take the next step toward that distance. Most leaders are really only good either at sharing the vision, or at guiding people along a path, but not both.

For example, many great theological and even congregational writers are only good at pointing to the horizon. They write and speak eloquently about where we "should" be going, what we "could" be doing, and how we "ought" to be living. But they aren't very good at telling people how to actually get there.

I've been somewhat surprised over my career at how many theologians write about church growth and vitality, without ever having led a church to that vitality; or at the number of pastors who've written about church growth after they've left the church, but before they ever tested their theories. These are people who are good at crafting a vision, but not so good at leading people along the path to that vision. They love to gaze at the horizon, at what could be, and try to convince others that this vision is the one to pursue. Unfortunately, if they cannot point out the pathway to start the journey, they create frustration. People may desperately want to go there, but they don't know how to get there.

I found this struggle with many of the books that I read in seminary. They were great at talking about where today's churches should be going: we should be more missional, we should be more pastoral, we should be more evangelical, we should be more . . . something that we aren't! But when I became a pastor I had no idea how to actually get people to do these things. I had been given a great vision, but no clarity on the steps to take toward that vision. And that's where most church-growth programs founder. They don't tell people how to get there, but boy do they point to a wonderful view.

Meanwhile, many, many pastors excel at pointing out the pathways, but they don't always know where they are going. Some try to lead their members back to a church that no longer exists. Their vision is the past. That doesn't mean that having a foot in our denomination's tradition isn't important. Our tradition tells us where we come from and what we don't want to lose. It's just that where we came from can't also be our destination.

Others aren't sure where they are leading us. They know the steps to take because they learned the steps from seminary classes and conferences. They know the things that they think they should be doing or ought to be doing, but in reality what they are doing is just taking steps. They lead their congregations to do all the things that churches typically do, that people think they ought to be doing, but they really have no vision in mind—only steps. These churches become lost because they don't know where they are going.

Like any journey, we have to know where we are going, but we also have to understand how to get there. Visionary leaders lead us to do both.

Proverb 55.

Some pastors and churches are called to do seeker evangelism. Some are called to do depth evangelism. Some are called to do hospice care. Some are called to do birthing. We need to be sure that we know what our leadership calling is.

NOT ALL CHURCHES HAVE THE SAME CALLING, but often we think that they should. Over the last twenty years, the most powerful influence on churches has been the emphasis on seeker evangelism—the focus on reaching out to the unchurched. This is an important calling for churches, and many of our modern megachurches excel at seeker evangelism.

Churches that excel at seeker evangelism assume that most of the people who don't go to church either didn't grow up in a church, or walked away from church because of a dislike of traditional churchism. So the emphasis is on creating churches that aren't like churches. Their worship areas may look like auditoriums or concert venues rather than like traditional sanctuaries. Typical religious art and artifacts are removed in favor of plants and creative projections on screens (much like the projections at rock concerts). Seats are auditorium style, and the front is often called "the stage," not the chancel or the altar. The music sounds like music heard on the radio, and the sermons are structured much like TED talks, self-help lectures, or infomercials. The small groups use materials meant for new Christians, and classes are designed to help people learn more about how to do faith. Everything is designed for those who are seekers—who have a very low level of religious education and understanding. But should every church be a seeker church and engage in seeker evangelism?

Our church engages in something we call "depth evangelism." We seek out seekers, but we seek out seekers of depth—people who want to grow to a deeper level of spiritual awareness and practice. So our sanctuary is much more traditional looking, filled with religious art, but also with some of the same sound, lighting, and projection abilities as the contemporary churches. We also have small groups and classes designed to move people to deeper levels of spiritual awareness and spiritual practices—groups that read works of great mystics and spiritual writers throughout Christian history, and that teach deeper levels of prayer, such as contemplative prayer. We know that we are trying to reach out to people who want a deeper spiritual life, even if they are skeptical of Christianity.

Some churches are social justice and mission churches. The words of their prayers, the sermons preached, the music chosen are all designed to get people involved in efforts to change the world. The groups and classes are designed to help people become more aware of the problems of the world and how we need to change them.

Other churches are more traditional. They are trying to maintain a traditional look, style, music, and aesthetic, all while being engaged in more traditional ministries. This isn't the same as saying that they are trapped in the 1950s and 1960s, although to some it may look that way. They update, but they are also trying to keep people rooted in more ancient, or at least more traditional practices.

Some churches are really hospices for people who are slowly dying away. At some point they were another kind of church, but they have since become hospice churches. They are places where the pastor is called upon to act like a chaplain, preaching and visiting those who are aging and struggling with age-related issues.

These are all just a few of the different kinds of churches that exist in the complex matrix of churches. Knowing what kind of church we are leading, and what kind of ministry we are called to as leaders, is important. It's hard to be a leader with one kind of calling leading a church with a different calling. For example, if our skills are in being caring and visiting, we're probably not going to do well in a seeker-style church. If we are a social justice pastor, we're probably not going to do as well in a traditional-style church. That doesn't mean that some aren't called to transform a church from one style to another. For example, my original calling for Calvin Presbyterian Church was to help transform a more traditional church into a more depth-oriented church, while also maintaining the church's emphasis on mission.

The key, as a leader, is understanding what our calling is, what our church's calling is, and trying to find a way to match our calling with its calling.

Proverb 56.

*Beware of mission creep because once your mission
starts creeping, it slows your ministry to a crawl.*

O NE OF THE THINGS THAT THE U.S. MILITARY has
become increasingly aware of since the Vietnam War,
but also because of many minor and major incur-
sions since then, is the danger of "mission creep." Mission
creep occurs when a clearly defined objective becomes blurry
because of a desire to engage in other missions that would be
good and helpful, but that aren't quite the original mission.

An example of this is the American incursion into Somalia in the early 1990s. The U.S. was part of a United Nations
peacekeeping effort during the Somalian civil war. They were
bringing desperately needed food into the country through
the port city of Mogadishu. The mission was clear: feed those
displaced by the war. But then the military's mission began
to creep. A local warlord, Mohamed Farrah Aidid, declared
himself president of the country and began to steal food
and medicine from the Red Cross. The U.S. military realized
that ridding the country of Aidid would be a good thing, so
it began to shift its mission. Instead of merely securing the
port and distributing food, they started hunting for the warlord in order to break his grip on the country. The results
were quite disastrous as the military became embroiled in a
poorly conceived, planned, and executed quest. It resulted
in the downing of a black hawk helicopter, and the capture
of its pilot, that eventually was chronicled in the film, *Black
Hawk Down*.

The hunt for Aidid was considered to be a noble cause
by many people worldwide, but because it wasn't part of
the original mission, and because it was hastily planned and

executed without really understating the topography, culture, context, and situation of Somalia and Mogadishu, it became disastrous. That was the creeping mission, and it brought the efforts in Somalia to a crawl.

Churches often engage in mission creep. They don't do it militarily, and the results aren't usually truly disastrous, but a creeping mission can kill the mission of a church. There are many, many things that a church can do, but it can't do all of them well. The point of any mission is to be clear about what the mission is, to stick to that mission, and only to veer from it when it seems that a tangential, related mission can be its own separate mission.

Where most churches creep is in piling on more and more mission on a particular mission effort. For example, a church may decide to raise money to repaint its sanctuary. In the process, someone suggests that repainting the sanctuary is being self-focused, and that it would be good to also raise money for the local food bank. Then someone notices that the storage area for the local food bank needs to be cleaned and repainted, so they decide to add in efforts to repaint and clean the food bank. In the process, they decide that it would be a good time to push for an effort to get more volunteers for the food bank. Who could complain about any of these goals?

So, when they try to raise funds to repaint the sanctuary, the church becomes disappointed by the sparse contributions. Why didn't more people contribute? All of those efforts were good, but the original mission was simply to repaint the sanctuary. That should have been the focus. The mission crept and became as much about the food bank as it did about the sanctuary. Let the raising of funds for the sanctuary be one effort. Let the food bank become a separate effort down the road. Focus on the mission at hand, and then create a new mission later when all the thinking, preparing, and contributing can be focused on that.

So many good ministry and mission efforts are sabotaged by the piling on of equally good ministry and mission efforts. Keep the mission from creeping, and the ministries and missions will have a good chance of flourishing.

Proverb 57.

*Learn the five attributes of great chefs, and
turn them into the five attributes of great pastors
and leaders: (1) They always use fresh ingredients.
(2) They work hard together behind the scenes
to make it look easy. (3) They are finicky
about cleanliness. (4) They always strive to
be hospitable and welcoming. (5) They are
passionate about feeding others.*

I'VE BEEN FASCINATED by what distinguishes great restaurants from good ones, and good ones from bad ones. Over time, just by observing and talking with those running good restaurants, I've noticed similarities between great restaurants. These are similarities that are equally valid in ministry. Great restaurants don't do everything great, but they do the basics really well. Churches can learn from this.

First, really great restaurants use fresh ingredients. The chefs pay attention to the quality of their food. Do our churches use fresh ingredients? What would fresh ingredients be in a church? It can be doing traditional rituals in a fresh way. It can be offering sermons where we're not just stuck behind a pulpit, reading a sermon that could have been written in the 1980s. It can mean offering different kinds of music, rather than just traditional church music. It can mean using small-group materials that don't just push an orthodox or traditional point of view, but offer a different way of looking at faith for people who don't see religion in the same way. Just as in every restaurant there are all sorts of foods that can be fresh, churches can present a whole variety of fresh offerings. The key is looking for freshness, not just being satisfied with the same old stale offerings that have always been offered.

Second, great restaurants work hard behind the scenes to make everything seem easy. They work hard on their coordination and communication. They expect cooks and servers and managers to communicate with each other, but in a cooperative way. Well-run restaurants don't have screaming in the kitchen, nor yelling, belittling, or constant criticism. They set high standards, but they help each other achieve those standards. Great churches are the same way. They set high standards, but they work cooperatively to achieve them. No one is the star. No one is the focus. Everyone finds a way to lift each other up. They don't snipe, criticize, or belittle. So the music director and the pastor work together to make worship great, rather than sniping about whose role is more important. The church leaders work together in budgeting to support each other's ministry, rather than having a "use it or lose it" mentality. If one committee struggles to find more money, another committee is willing to cut their own budget to support the other. The education and youth people work together to create good programs. Yet from the outside it seems like everything works effortlessly. That's the evidence of good work behind the scenes: it doesn't look like work.

Third, they are finicky about cleanliness. No one wants to eat in a dirty restaurant where the floors are dirty, tables are sticky, bathrooms are smelly, and the décor is musty. No one wants to worship in a church where floors are dirty, pews or seats are grubby, the bathrooms are smelly, and the sanctuary seems musty.

Fourth, great restaurants strive to be welcoming and hospitable. They aren't overbearing. They don't cling. Nor do they ignore. They are appropriate, welcoming people to the restaurant, helping them find a table, seeing if there's any way to help, and making the experience one where the focus can actually be on the food. Churches also need to be welcoming and hospitable. Many churches think they are, but they aren't. They are hospitable to those they know, but often they ignore those they don't know. They don't welcome visitors and help them find a place to sit. With sanctuary seating, they can be like the old fogey restaurant where long-time customers walk in, see someone in their normal table, sniff snottily, and complain that the service isn't what it used to be. Great restaurants help everyone feel welcome.

Finally, great restaurants are passionate about feeding people. Great restaurateurs are passionate about food. Great church leaders are passionate about God, faith, and a life of service. They want people to have revelational experiences in church. They want people to be transformed in the same way that eating in a great restaurant can feel revelational and transforming. And they put their passion to everything as much as possible: to preaching, teaching, leading, creating, forming, guiding, counseling, and everything else. Not everything they do can be great, but they can try to be passionate in all they do.

Ultimately, great restaurants help us dig out of the doldrums to realize that there is something better possible. And they make us look forward to returning. Great churches are the same way.

Proverb 58.

Healthy churches need to be both goal-oriented and God-oriented. Being goal-oriented means we see where we are going and what steps need to be taken to get there. Being God-oriented means we pay attention to where God is calling us to go so that we become goal-oriented in seeking God's orientation.

IT'S THE STANDARD PRACTICE IN BUSINESSES, organizations, and even churches to be goal-oriented. Whether it's engaging in long-range planning, setting sales objectives, creating production schedules and the like, the focus is often on creating certainty and planning for the future.

Churches, over the years, have tried to adopt these principles to congregations, setting one-, three-, and five-year plans for growth—often to mixed results. It makes sense, though, to try to bring these principles into the church. Why not? Aren't churches really just businesses, selling Jesus as their product? Especially with newer churches, don't they try to market themselves to a spiritually hungry, yet often finicky, market? Doesn't it make sense to bring in principles that get churches to become more focused on customer satisfaction, efficiency, and greater production of programs to meet the customers' needs? Doesn't it make sense to create goal-oriented plans that propel growth into the future?

Uh, no. Why not? Because churches aren't businesses. In fact, they are entities unto themselves. They are similar to businesses, but they are also similar to government (varying between democratic or more authoritarian rule), community organizations, and families. They are similar to a lot of entities, but that doesn't make them those entities.

There's nothing wrong with being goal-oriented in a church, but it can't come at the expense of being God-oriented first. When church members, leaders, and pastors make business principles a primary focus, it becomes too easy to push God to the margins. We become functional and slowly diminish the spiritual, which is what's happening in too many of our struggling, and even growing, churches. For instance, some of the most successful churches (in terms of growth, at least) get so good at using business principles that their churches become monuments to market-driven growth. Meanwhile, struggling churches often grasp at straws, trying any organizational principle that might help them grow, but then become discouraged and push God to the margins because nothing seems to work and conflict grows.

Whatever principles we use to operate a church, we are called to be God-oriented above all. That's the model of the gospels and of Acts. Jesus always sought the Father's will first and was always led by the Spirit. I am fairly certain that he had goals and a plan, but he always started with seeking what the Father wanted. The goals and plans served God's calling. The same can be said about the apostles. They started with a God-orientation, and allowed their goals and plans to flow out of that.

The key is that if we are only goal-oriented without being God-oriented, then we end up becoming exactly what we know isn't right—a business marketing God. That may allow us to grow in numbers, but it will also cause us to shrink in Spirit.

Proverb 59.

*We can only think things through theologically
and liturgically if we start by thinking things through
spiritually and psychologically, which is where
we create the possibility for a deep encounter
with God in worship.*

AMONG PROTESTANTS THE KEY WORD is always "theology." To borrow a phrase from Freud, for us theology is the royal road. In virtually every denomination we train people for ministry by sending them to "theological" seminaries. We articulate our positions and beliefs in theological language. We debate our theological positions. Our websites tell people what we believe, even if they are more interested in understanding why we believe. There's an unwritten, and often unwitting, belief among many Protestants that our primary goal is to develop the "right" theology.

In fact, if there is a Protestant equivalent to the Catholic problem of "works righteousness" (the belief that we can save ourselves by doing good deeds that merit God's grace), it is the problem of "beliefs righteousness" (the belief that by having the right beliefs we can merit God's grace). No one would really admit to this out loud, but we Protestants hold a secret belief that if we can get our church and members to have the right theological beliefs, it will lead us to form a healthy and growing church and ministry.

For example, many conservative Christians believe that it is a greater acceptance of a progressive theology that has led to the decline of the mainline. In effect, because our theology is wrong we've lost God's grace. Meanwhile, many progressive Christians believe that if only our theology was more inclusive, more compassionate, and less legalistic, people would flock to our churches. They see decline as arising out of an overly exclusive theology that leads people to walk away from religion. The reality is that churches of all theologies are shrinking, and a minority of churches, representing a variety of theologies, is growing. Could it be that other factors come into play?

I discovered how engrained *beliefs righteousness* is in my own denomination back in the early 1990s, when I met the moderator of our denomination. I asked him why he thought that our denomination was shrinking. He replied, "Because we don't think theologically enough. If we could get people to think theologically in the right way, the rest would take care of itself." It is now twenty-four years later, and it seems like all our denominations do is debate who has the right theology. What does it look like to get people to think theologically in the "right" way? What's the objective measurement of a "right" theological belief?

In reality, we spend so much time trying to get our theology right that we generally ignore the need to get our psychology and spirituality right. People don't live life first from a rational, analytical, theological perspective. They live life at the level of physical, psychological, and relational experiences. And they come to church seeking psychological insights that lead to spiritual experiences of God, love, and joy. Rarely do people come to church seeking the right theology—the exception being those who seek out only those churches that already think like them. Most people come hoping to encounter and experience God. Even more, they hope that these experiences will help get their lives in order so that they can deal with the conflict, turmoil, and uncertainties of those lives. They aren't looking for right beliefs. They are looking for how to form a right spirit that leads to a better life.

Let's be clear: as I've stated many times before, theological beliefs are crucial in helping us understand God, life, and purpose. Still, theology follows spirituality. The experience of God comes first. Theological reflection comes later. Theology is wonderful in helping us understand our experiences, as well as the insights and experiences of those in the Bible. It gives us tremendous insight into life that leads to a deeper spirit. Still, when theological constructs, concepts, and doctrine become a substitute for the encounter with God—when we live in our heads thinking *about* God, while never really connecting *with* God—we end up with an abstract, disconnected, and fruitless theology.

When it comes to worship especially, we need to start first with people's psychological and spiritual yearnings and experiences. Does the music we play and sing open people up to an encounter with God, close them off, or leave them numb? Do our sermons lead people to an encounter with God, giving them guidance on how to live, or are they theological treatises that might appeal to our former seminary professors, while leaving worshippers feeling empty?

Starting at the theological level means focusing on what we think is "right" worship first, and then constructing worship from there without ever asking or caring what people are experiencing. It leads us to get caught up in discussions on whether people should clap in church (because, after all, worship should be God-focused, not us-focused); whether we are doing communion in the right way (because, after all, Jesus never did communion by intinction); whether we are offering the right music (because, after all, God likes classical worship music best—*someone actually said that to me, once*); whether we are teaching people the right evangelical, classical, Reformed, Lutheran, Wesleyan, or progressive theology in our sermons (because, after all, getting our theology right is all that matters).

Starting at the psychological and spiritual level means asking first what people are experiencing when they worship. Are they experiencing God, or something else? This doesn't just mean focusing on the experiences of the people who've always been there. We need to ask where other worshippers are in their psychological maturity. Where are they in their spiritual awareness? Are they craving a traditional approach to worship? Are they craving a more contemporary approach? Are they craving something else? Are we creative enough to offer something else? Are they just there to fill up their time and be in the right place to feel saved? Are they seeking something deeper? Are we taking time to find out what their perceptions are? Are we taking time to adjust ourselves to where they are so that we can help them grow spiritually and theologically?

The ultimate question is whether people are having the kind of personal experiences that lead to a connection with God, and that then leads them to want to learn a theology of God that deepens their experiences? When we start with experiences, it can lead to a desire for a clearer and deeper foundation of beliefs. But when we start with a foundation of beliefs, it can act like a closed door with a sign on it, saying, "Only those who believe what we believe are welcome."

Proverb 60.

Good leadership means being able to be obsessive, improvising, and laid back all at the same time. Real wisdom comes with knowing when to be what.

OVER THE YEARS I'VE HAD THE OPPORTUNITY to work with many pastors and seminary students as a spiritual director, mentor, supervisor, head of staff, and teacher. I've been gratified to see some really succeed and soar, and disappointed to see others struggle and sink.

What's been the difference between them? Those who've soared seemed to have had a natural, intuitive ability to balance how they respond to different situations. Those who've sunk seemed to have only one way to respond to everything.

What's the balance? Those who've soared are detail-focused enough to set high standards. When it's called for, they are also content to improvisationally fly by the seat of their pants, especially when things don't work according to plan. At the same time, they are relaxed enough in any moment that they don't let failed plans and uncertainty about what to do drive them crazy, nor cause them to act crazily.

Unfortunately, those who've sunk have tended to be *either* obsessive, improvisational, or laid back in any situation. For example, I've come across many pastors who are just obsessive. They anxiously fret about all the details of the church. As a result, they erode their relationships by demanding too much from others, while simultaneously complaining that nobody steps up to help them. They never realize that nobody steps up to help the person who does everything. Why? Because that person never really lets anyone else do anything, even when they try to let go. The obsessive person will watch the other nervously, and the step in, saying, "You're not doing that right." It's like the friend of mine who complained that her husband didn't hold the baby enough. Later I saw him holding the baby, and then saw her snatch the baby from his arms, saying, "You're not holding him right!"

Pastors like this often long to let go, but they can't. And it's reflected in their preaching, too. They worry so much about having the perfect wording that their sermons become overly detailed, dry, and impersonal. It's like listening to a professor read a paper in public.

Meanwhile, there are some pastoral leaders who are so laid back in everything that the church becomes chaotic. Meetings with them are frustrating because there's never clarity about what to do, or organization around how to do it. The people around them may step up to organize, but they constantly feel guilty because they wonder if they are overstepping boundaries. Their preaching is confusing, too, because there never seems to be a point. Just a laid back, friendly set of stories or thoughts.

Finally, there are some pastors who are great at flying by the seat of their pants, calmly coming up with spontaneously creative solutions to any situation. Yet they lead the people around them into paralysis as they try to figure out what they should do. These pastors never quite let others know what they are doing—mainly because it's all being made up as things go along. Their preaching is also disjointed as they go from idea to idea, like a hummingbird among flowers.

When we are just one of these, or even just two of these, we become like a carpenter with only one or two tools. We need more than that. The key to good leadership is being able to balance all three, and having the wisdom to know when to be what.

This balance is hard to explain concretely, but I can give one example. Years ago our seminary intern planned a children's sermon using a song on a CD. Our worship computer wouldn't play the CD. What to do, what do to? So we asked the music director if he knew the song and could play it? He didn't. The intern had a panic-stricken look on her face as her carefully planned children's sermon crumbled before her.

I stood up and asked, jokingly, if anyone knew the song. No one did. Then I asked if anyone knew where we could find portable CD player in the church. Someone in the back said that she saw one downstairs in a classroom. I said, "Go get it," and then asked the piano player to play a waiting song. He played the theme from Jeopardy. I then asked, "Anyone know a hymn that's good for waiting?" Someone suggested a hymn I've now long forgotten. Halfway through the verse the person with the CD player ran in. We plugged it in, the seminary intern did her children's sermon, and people thought it was the greatest thing ever.

Begin obsessive would have meant becoming frustrated and defeated when the computer wouldn't work. Being laid back would have meant skipping the children's sermon and just moving on. Being improvisational would have meant doing something else. We did all three. We stuck with the plan, improvised the waiting time for a fix to the problem, and were laid back enough to find it all fun.

Wisdom lies in the balance of the three.

www.ingramcontent.com/pod-product-compliance
Lightning Source LLC
Jackson TN
JSHW081317130125
77033JS00011B/323

* 9 7 8 0 8 1 9 2 3 2 8 2 3 *